Systems Theory

OVER 125 SYSTEMS INSIDE!

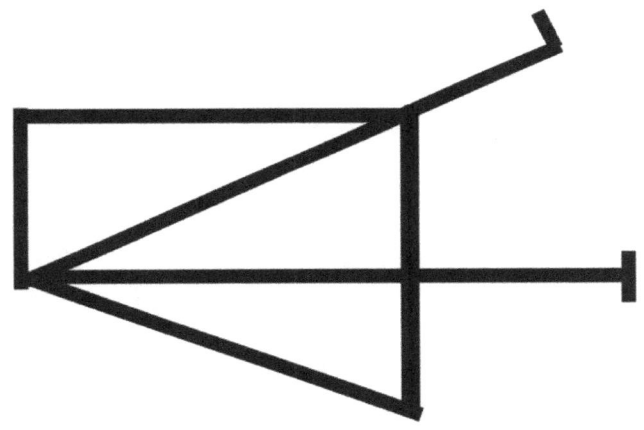

Nathan Coppedge

SYSTEMS THEORY

(Formal-, applied-, rubric-, etc.)

by Nathan Coppedge

Nathan Coppedge

SYSTEMS THEORY

A had a friend who had a theory that 'systems can be formed about anything.' And initially I resisted, but more and more I am convinced of the validity of this point of view.

23 FORMAL / LOGICAL SYSTEMS

Traditionally it is said that no more than 8 of these major logical systems could be formed, some of which may not have been found. However, here I present a concept of 19 of them.

Analogy————————————p.17

Neology————————————p. 19

Thoughtful Socrates—————————p. 22

Syllogisms—————————————p. 27

Mathematics————————————-p. 29

Iota Logic (Equational Logic)————-p. 36

Arbitrary Mathematics———————-p. 39

Para-Lemma Logic————————-p. 42

Meta-Mathematics————————-p. 48

Logical Methodology ————————-p. 53

Categorical Deduction——————-p. 54

Method of Solving Paradoxes————-p. 58

Principle-Puzzle————————-p. 66

The Vesselext—————————p. 70

AOLT-There——————————p. 76

Exceptionism—————————-p. 81

Ametaph———————————p. 83

Qualifics———————————-p. 87

Entics————————————p. 92

Irrational Logic—————————p. 98

Problematics —————————p. 103

Eridian Leap ——————————p. 104

Genius ————————————p. 105

4 MEANING SYSTEMS

Affirmativism ——————————p. 109

Authenticity ——————————p. 110

Abridgement ——————————-p. 111

Systems Theory

Anything Theory —————————— p. 112

5 TRUTH SYSTEMS

Veridication————————————p. 115

Braid of Correspondences—————p. 116

Prescriptions ————————————— p. 121

Acquisition Theory ————————p. 122

Metaphysical Perspectivism ————p. 123

5 ARCHETYPAL SYSTEMS

Square Tooth Systems——————————p. 127

Jagged Tooth Systems——————————p. 128

Close Logic——————————————p. 130

Far Logic————————————————p. 132

Archetypal Root Expansion————p. 134

4 META THEORIES

Meta-Criticism————————————p. 137

Broken Systems————————————p. 139

False Systems ——————————p. 140

Metaphysics I. ————————————p. 144

14 QUALIFIED ETHICAL SYSTEMS

Egalitarianism ————————————p. 153

Karmaband ————————————p. 154

Wisdom ————————————p. 158

Directionality ————————————p.160

Selective Ethics ————————————p. 162

The Disputation ————————————p. 180

Hypocritical Knowledge ——————p. 190

Metaphysics II ————————————p. 193

Doxologic ————————————p. 198

Planar Transcendence ——————————p. 203

Imparallel Realization——————————p. 205

Intellectual Morals ————————————p. 206

Exceptional Morality ——————— p. 207

Priesthood 1 ————————————p. 208

Systems Theory

1 IMMORTAL SYSTEM

Usineosis————————————p. 211

8 QUALIFIED METAPHYSICAL SYSTEMS

Ersatz Metaphysics——————————p. 215

The Norma————————————p. 216

Philosophical Realism——————————p. 218

Wizard Metaphysics——————————p. 219

Statues Model ————————————p. 221

Non-Identity Theory ————————p. 222

String Theory ————————————p. 223

Plenum-Not-Planet Theory————————p. 224

22 APPLIED SYSTEMS

Advanced Concept Analysis————————p. 227

Original Geography——————————p. 229

Macroscopy————————————p. 230

Basic Property Analysis————————p. 232

Idea Mechanics ————————————p. 233

Newton's Laws of Motion————p. 235

The Laws of Thermodynamics ——p. 236

Weapon Systems ————————p. 237

Public Works—————————p. 241

Visual Parsing————————p. 244

Volitional Mechanics—————p. 247

Qualifactics—————————p. 250

Semaphores—————————p. 256

Inflectionism—————————p. 258

Kinetic Metaphor———————p. 259

Brain Repair—————————p. 260

Choice Selection Theory————p. 261

Active Process ———————p. 262

Intelligence Analysis —————p. 263

Virtuitics ——————————p. 264

Standard Critique ——————p. 265

Exceptional Replacement ——p. 266

Systems Theory

1 DRAMATIC SYSTEM

Dramatic Lessons————————-p. 269

7 PSYCHOLOGICAL SYSTEMS

Infantile Psychology————————-p. 275

Mainstream Psychology————————p. 278

Harmonizing————————————p. 282

Individuation————————-p. 286

Gestalt Theory————————-p. 288

Mnemosis————————p. 289

Epoctics————————————-p. 291

1 PHENOMENOLOGICAL SYSTEM

Phenomenology————————p. 297

5 AESTHETIC SYSTEMS

Archetypal Aesthetics ————————p. 301

Hyper-Landscape————————p. 302

Game Aesthetics————————-p. 304

11

Impossible Problems ——————p. 307

The Metaphysical Art——————p. 308

4 SENSE SYSTEMS

The 5 Senses——————————p. 313

The Sixth Sense ————————p.314

Telesis ————————————p. 323

Inherent Vision ————————p. 324

7 RUBRIC SYSTEMS

Hierarchy of Biology——————p. 329

Functional Hierarchy——————p. 330

Food Pyramid—————————p. 332

Quality Control————————p. 333

Epicurean Body Types—————p. 334

Formal Standards———————p. 335

Hours of Inspiration———————p. 337

Systems Theory

13 MAGICAL SYSTEMS

"Ken" ——————————————————p. 341

Alchemy ———————————— p. 343

Incantation ——————————————p. 348

Chi Power ——————————————p. 350

Enchantment ——————————————p. 352

Wormholes ——————————————p. 354

Aura Reading ——————————————p. 355

Psychic Prediction ——————————p. 356

Objects of Influence ————————————p. 365

Magical Rumination ————————————p. 366

Apocryphal Prophecy ———————————p. 367

Premonition ————————————— p. 369

Mysteries ———————————— p.370

3 RELIGIOUS SYSTEMS

Asceticism ——————————————p. 373

Epicureanism ——————————————p. 375

Asceticureanism ———————————— p. 377

5 PROGRAMMABLE SYSTEMS

Object-Oriented Programming ——p. 381

Coherent Logic Program ————-p. 382

Branding Program ——————p. 391

Ancient Book Design Program ——-p. 393

Scripted Functions ——————p. 395

3 INTERFACE SYSTEMS

Open-and-Closed Logic ———— p. 399

Expansion Models ——————p. 400

"Watering-hole" Strategies ———-p. 401

APPENDIX 1 ——————— p. 405

RECOMMENDED READING ——-P. 407

BIOGRAPHY ——————p. 410

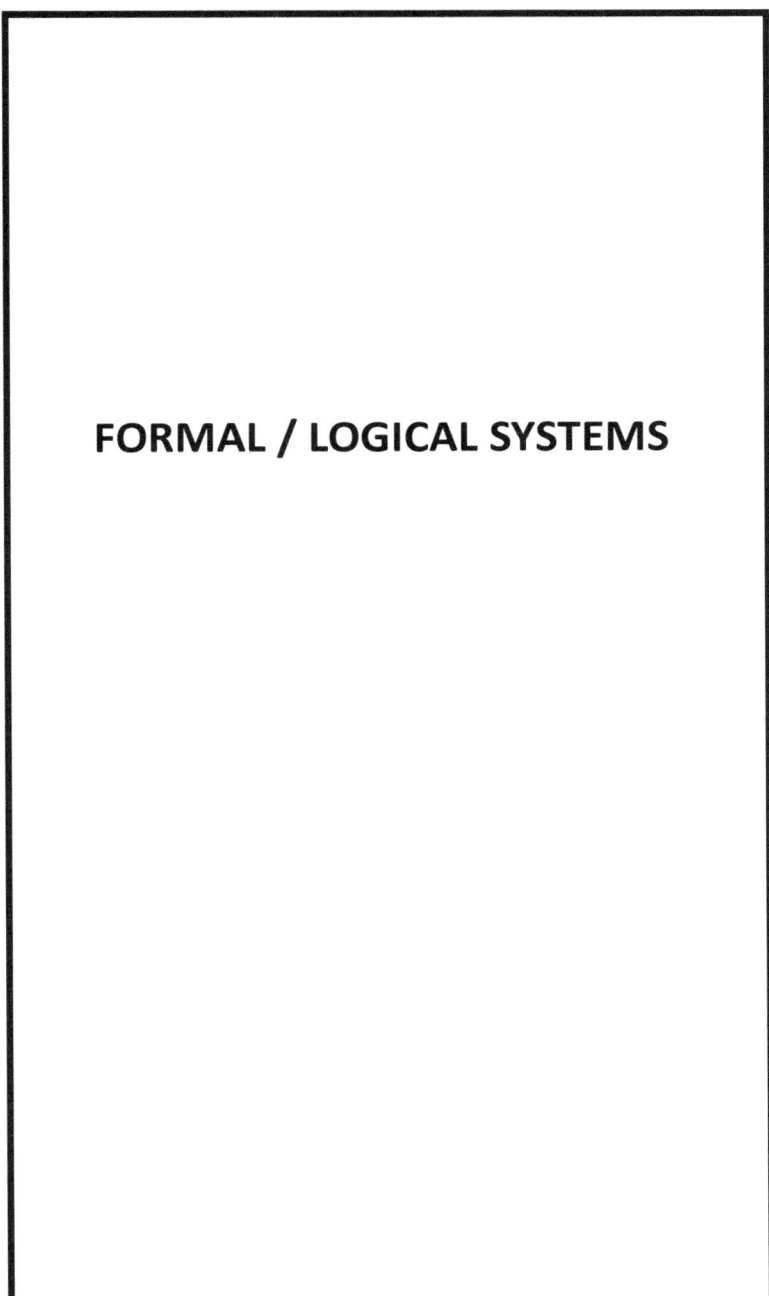

FORMAL / LOGICAL SYSTEMS

Nathan Coppedge

Systems Theory

FORMAL / LOGICAL SYSTEMS

ANALOGIES

An analogy takes the form of an informal comparison of

opposites, in which opposites are compared directly.

For example, "Cat: Mouse :: Dog : Cat"

Reads: "Cat is to mouse just as dog is to cat".

Cat and mouse are informal opposites, and so are
dog and cat.

Furthermore, each opposite pair must have a certain express

relationship, and the relationship must be of the
same character

for the overall comparison to qualify as an analogy.

So, for example, although we might assume this works:

"Mouse : Dog :: Large cat : Small cat" in fact this doesn't work,

because the cats might be friends, or the dog might not attack

mice like cats do.

In general, analogies are limited by what I call 'modal' relationships. That is, they 'just happen to be the case' therefore, they do not have universal significance.

We cannot say, for example, that a hateful dog loves cats, even though we can say that hate is the opposite of love, and dog is the MODAL opposite of cats. This terminology was developed later by Nathan Coppedge to explain the difference be-tween analogies and categorical deductions. Cate-gorical deductions, by contrast, DO CLAIM univer-sality.

Systems Theory

FORMAL / LOGICAL SYSTEMS

NEO-LOGIC

Neo-Logic, or formerly, neology or neologism, is the use of words

and word parts to define new concepts. These words and

word-parts may be called 'concepts' and 'particles'.

Common concepts and particles in logic and philosophy include:

Meta-	-Physical	-Science
Super-	-Theoretical	-Ology
Macro-	-Sophy	-Logic
Micro-	-Mathematics	-X theory

The words and word-labels may also include the names of

pre-existing disciplines such as biology, astronomy, and linguistics.

In an applied sense, any neological 'identity' may also relate with

a further Y property after it concerns X theory, leading to many branches of complexity, typically with no greater depth than four or five outside of the composite definition of the identity, and the single level of elaboration at the open-ended level (e.g. such as a formal paper).

I have used neology to define a number of concepts, including:

*Metemphysics: The science of the physicalism of ideas.

*Macrosophy: The study of what is philosophically large.

*Microsophy: The study of what is philosophically small.

*Axiometry: The coherent geometry of axioms.

*Antialethianism: The way gods find meaning in meaninglessness.

I have also had a role in defining or contributing to pre-existing

neological areas, such as:

Systems Theory

*Sophology or Sophiology: Theories about theories.

*Ontography: Describing the world objectively.

*Weather Studies: Philosophy or discursions about weather.

*Proportional or Ordinal Numbers: Post-rational numbers.

*Entiology: Study of entities.

FORMAL / LOGICAL SYSTEMS

SOCRATIC METHOD / SOCRATIC THOUGHT

Socrates, although little is remembered of him, has a majority in the significance of ideas. His admirer, Plato, virtually invented ideas. That suggests a potency that is super-ordinary, as his place in Plato's life was very singular on that subject. Socrates asked large questions, and made use of the strategy of deep implication.

For example, metaphysics was an analysis. That is a Socratic statement.

This could be developed (if one had the mind to do so) into a deep

implication:

metaphysics was an analysis --->

The question of the universal world --->

Maybe the world isn't universal.

This is already the Copernican revolution.

However, notice how this thought, easily managed

Systems Theory

by Socrates,

suggests a total eclipse of prior beliefs.

Analogize, and nature becomes naturalism
(another Socratic thought), but this is merely sup-
plementary, because the idea is had by Socrates.
This would be considered fundamental for understanding.

The universe or concept of a larger world would in
the sense of these prior aspects be considered as
a possible one-to-one analysis, which could in turn
be considered as a metaphor, or again metaphysics, or some other new idea emerging from the old
---another Socratic idea similar to dialectical materialism and evolution.

As Socrates is presumed to have jumped into each
topic independently, as though he were a different
person, he was in fact the same person, the best
philosophical person.

If there is something missing, it is the failure of
other people to preserve his complete influence.

An additional Socratic pursuit:

Every assumption is wrong in some way.

We act creatively to interpret any one thing --- then we are somewhere else!

That location has NO location!

That second location is the real location, the location called NO LOCATION.

I can argue that when we understand everything, we understand

NOTHING.

Everything is nothing, in that second location.

However, right HERE, where we ARE, there IS NO TRUTH.

We cannot KNOW unless we GO THERE.

THERE IS NOWHERE!

[Divinatory note: but think of it as an acronym. Focus on the first part first, and the last part last----].

ADDITIONALLY,

WHAT IS JUSTICE FOR SOCRATES?

I don't know.

But, I have written something fairly significant on Socrates (at least I think so).

Based on my writing, I can attempt to surmise the following:

1.Socrates' first view might be the premise that Justice is from the gods.

2.Socrates would then argue that if the gods are just, so be it.

3.Socrates might then argue that only one of the gods is named Justice.

4.Socrates might then make an expostulation about how divine justice might be different from justice for mortals.

5.At this point it explodes into a lot of different questions, like 'is Justice absolute?' 'Does Justice rule over mortals?' and 'Does Justice rule justly?' The conclusion leads back to answering the question of whether divine justice is different than justice for mortals.

6.Socrates now raises the question of 'What is justice for mortals?' Since we cannot know divine justice, we must concern ourselves with justice of this kind.

7.Justice for mortals must be some relative kind of justice. It is not justice at all, but an appearance of justice.

8.If justice is the appearance of justice then we must concern ourselves with the good life, for the good life is all that has the appearance of justice.

That's my sense of it.

Systems Theory

FORMAL / LOGICAL SYSTEMS

SYLLOGISMS

Also known as logical syllogisms, these are a form of deduction originally arranged by Aristotle. They come in a wide variety of forms, but only a small number are logically valid.

The two most common are Modus Ponens and Hypothetical Inference.

Modus Ponens:	Hypothetical Inference:
All systems are logical.	If I drink will become drunk.
A is a system	I am drunk.
A must be logical.	Therefore, I took a drink.

In both forms, the soundness of the conclusion (s) depends on the soundness of all of the premises related with the conclusion.

Syllogisms may be called causal forms of inference, because the conclusions usually depend on more than one premise, and there is no rule which says that conclusions cannot contradict one another.

Since the system cannot be proven coherent, it must be assumed that the conclusions are derived from the nature of the premises exclusively, as numerous philosophers have emphasized in the last 100 years.

For an example of coherent deduction, see Categorical Deduction.

The difference may be criticized as a distinction between empirical premises and systematic ones, and depending on the types of logical biases, one or another may be deemed more or less trivial than the other.

Systems Theory

FORMAL / LOGICAL SYSTEMS

MATHEMATICS

Decimal System

1 . = one

2 .. = two

3 ... = three

4 . . . . = four

5 . . . . . = five

6 . . . . . . = six

7 . . . . = seven

8 . . . . = eight

9 . . . . = nine

10 = 9 + 1 = ten

20 = 10 + 10 = twenty

30 = 20 + 10 = thirty

40 = 20 + 20 = forty

50 = 30 + 20 = fifty

60 = 40 + 20 = sixty

70 = 50 + 20 = seventy

80 = 40 + 40 = eighty

90 = 50 + 40 = ninety

100 = one hundred (90 + 10)

200 = two hundred (100 + 100)

1000 = one thousand (500 + 500)

1,000,000 = one million (1000 * 1000)

Infinitesimal numbers = 0.00000000000...1

0.00000000000...2 etc.

0.11111111111...1 etc.

0.99999999999...9

These are small, infinitely repeating numbers.

Rational numbers.

These are numbers with values expressible in fractions and mathematical relationships.

X = any number.

Y = any number, possibly different from X.

Systems Theory

Z= any number, possibly different from X and Y

10X = 10 of any number.

X / Y = Any number divided by any number.

3X / Y = Any number divided by any number

in which X tends to be three times larger than Y.

Equations

1 + 1 = 2

2 + 3 = 5

2 * 10 = 20

1 / 10 = 0.1

1/100 = 0.01

1/1000 = 0.001

10 / 20 = 1/2 = 0.5

10X = Y = Y is exactly 10 * X

That is the same as writing 10X - Y = 0.

Squares and Square Roots

0 ^ 1 = 0 * 1 = 0

1 ^ 0 = 1 * 1 = 1

2 ^ 0 = 1 * 1 * 1 = 1 etc.

1 ^ 2 = 1 * 1 = 1

1 ^ 3 = 1 * 1 * 1 = 1

2 ^ 2 = 2 * 2 = 4

2 ^ 3 = 2 * 2 * 2 = 8

1 root of any number is that number.

The 2 root of any number is the square root of that number.

The square root of 4 is 2, because two 2s multiply to equal 4.

Number	Sq. Rt.
4	2
9	3
16	4
25	5
36	6
49	7
64	8

Systems Theory

Scientific Notation

$1 \times 10^1 = 10$

$1 \times 10^2 = 100$

$1 \times 10^3 = 1000$

$1 \times 10^4 = 10,000$

$1 \times 10^5 = 100,000$

$1 \times 10^6 = 1,000,000$ etc.

Trans-Finite Numbers

$1/0 = \text{Infinity}$

$2/0 = 2 * \text{Infinity} = \text{Infinity}$

$\text{Infinity} * \text{Infinity} = \text{Infinity}$

$\text{Infinity} / 2 = \text{Infinity}$

Differential Calculus, (Part I.)

Calculus is stupid. Calculus is for extroverts. It's either totally easy, or you learn calculus. Calculus is about thinking —-wait that's for philosophers.

The origin is a variable. The derivative is the angle of a line —- that's a small thing somehow, however, isn't it? The process might be unlimited. Even the opposite mathematics has its limits. It also may have no function. There are no opposites in calculus: there are only functions. Structures are imaginary. Applied calculus is the tough part—for which you have your handy calculator.

You can't be on the side of calculus—- Calculus just IS. One thing to know is that calculus always has a power. If you input zero you get zero, just like in algebra.

Advanced concepts in calculus: 1. Everything of value is outside calculus. 2. Maybe +3. 3. Calculus for all integers. That's just an idea. It's arbitrary in God's logic is one of the first things I learned. Even now in calculus there is a division between professors who teach calculus as intuition and those that teach it as pure mathematics. Ultimately there may be more than one way to do calculus but remember, calculus is stupid , or you're a genius.

Towards the end of his life, Leibniz lamented: what's human about calculus? So, calculus does have a downside. I'll leave that as a puzzle.

Systems Theory

Integral Calculus (Part II.)

Wrong! Doubly wrong! Specifics don't matter. Form a hypothesis, then throw it away! Apply the existing hypothesis, be conventional. Get it right! It concerns science! Be scientific! Clouds are clocks! Simplify always! Stay distanced from your work. Or pull an Einstein. Know. Philosophy is contraband. The rest is history.

Posterior Calculus (Part IIi.)

Now, I told you it wasn't about philosophy, but it is! All you need to know at first is Delta V. Whatever you interpret from is analytic a posteriori. Because you know you will get what results—- You have to begin somewhere, so you begin with the effect of an unseen cause. The cause is analytic. Delta V. is when you attach an effect to a cause—- And you call it —- what do you call it? Analytic. The rest is logic… I'm sure you can figure it out. It depends on the case.

Concluding Remarks

Sometimes we think calculus is a disease. Sometimes we think it is not logical at all. But mostly we think it is a highly useful thinking tool. Perhaps you'll side with the Leibniz who thought it was inhuman, or perhaps you'll side with the Leibniz who brought it upon himself to invent calculus.

FORMAL / LOGICAL SYSTEMS

IOTA LOGIC / EQUATIONAL LOGIC

Certain logical operators work both as variables and as operators. Thus, when they are used together, they can be used
without changing any of the other operators within the equation.

The only form of commutation necessary is where the sign is
located in relation to the equals sign. These signs include
equals, but also a number of signs I have invented, including:

[Colophon Symbol]

Colon to the left: Automatically reach left answer.

Colon to the right: Multiply every term left by right.

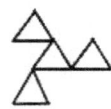

[Akhenaton Symbol]: Third wheels.

E.g. with brackets afterwards or a colon

to the left or right.

[God Variable]: Infinity + 1 or any value

Systems Theory

including infinity for each variable.

[Demi-God Variable]: God, exception

conditions cannot be met. All variables are

undefined, or value is less than negative

infinity.

[Dragon Symbol]

For every dragon there is an infinite iteration.

[Theophrastus Symbol]

A way of introducing logical conjectures to

mathematics (x = y theophrastus : conjecture).

Also included are a selection of logical symbols such as:

(Necessary Conditional, Coherency, Sometimes, and Ambigute)...

So, for example,

$$| \; \text{Ƿ} \quad : +10 \; | \; = \text{increment a previous}$$

answer 10.

OR (Another example...)

$$\text{All} \; \oplus \; _{\{a,b,c...n\}} \quad \vDash \; \oplus \; _f \; \in \; x$$

E.g. because a coherent function contains all data.

OR,

$$\oplus \; \vDash \; _{\{if\}} \; \in \; _{Inf.} \; \ast$$

E.g. because a coherent function of i contains all possibilities.

More in the as-yet-unpublished Dimensional Mathematics Toolkit, by Nathan Coppedge.

Systems Theory

FORMAL / LOGICAL SYSTEMS

ARBITRARY MATHEMATICS

Seminal Work on Math Expanded for Larger Formal Systems

Pre-requisite: 2-d decimal system.

Zero can have an area.

Multiple origins are possible.

Arbitrary mathematics.

(Not just numbers, but also other formal ideas:

not-just-number theory)

As in philosophy, there is a need to define the rules.

However, the rules can be mathematical.

They can also be logical, where logic permits.

In arbitrary mathematics, the biggest assumptions are logical.

The biggest products are linguistic, chemical, biological, historical, fictional, etc.

A model to uphold is the concept of a theoretic paradigm.

The modification of the theoretical paradigm leads to different 'worlds'.

As in Modal Realism, the worlds are different from one another in at least one way (whatever way that may be), but unlike MR, the differences are purely theoretical.

In fact, in any given study of arbitrary mathematics, it may be that only one world is considered: the world under which the specific model of rules holds.

Since the theory is so broad, it may be helpful to consider problems first. The extent to which problem-conditions are accepted can become a model for functions.

Another possibility is to consider functions first. If functions can be based on problems, then positing functions may be just as strong as positing problems. Functions have the advantage that they are not necessarily problematic.

Systems Theory

Thus, the ideal system can be based on functions.

If a particular system of functions is especially strong, then it defines a particular set of rules, and it is back to problems.

Problems define functions define systems which define problems.

All of this regardless of whether math is the only system involved.

FORMAL / LOGICAL SYSTEMS

PARA-LEMMA LOGIC

Part I.

Mathematical and Exceptional Lemmas

Initially, para-lemma logic exists in two senses:

1. The sense of mathematics / primary Lemma Logic

* Necessary by theory (T = Theory)

** Math for philosophers (BAD)

*** Advanced math (GOOD)

**** Einstein-only (?)

***** Too crazy (MADEN)

2. The sense of qualifying the lemma

Systems Theory

For example, in a set of lemma statements:

1

1*

2

2*

2.5

2.5*

Or the like, lemmas can be used to act retroactively
upon the logical relations of statements in a list.
This is only arbitrary if the list is arbitrary, which
may be seen as the first rule of para-lemma logic.

We can see relations such as:

1 : 2 :: 1* : 2*

And similarly,

1 : 2* :: 3* : 4**

The clear distinction is that stars always relate with
stars, that is, it is impossible to reach a comparison
like this:

1 : 2* :: 3 : 4, which would be illegal.

So, that may serve as the second rule.

A star always produces a star within the direct comparison, or otherwise across from the compari-son. So, we get four major types of comparisons assuming four numbers and up to four lemmas:

1 : 2 :: 3 : 4

1 : 1* :: 2 : 2*

1* : 2* :: 3* : 4* (or, also: 1** : 2** :: 3** : 4**)

1* : 2** :: 3** : 4***

The advanced level (in Para-Lemma Logic) is to use the logical relationships created by the original variables to construct meanings for the lemmas themselves.

For example, the most basic level might be:

A : B :: C : D = No Lemma.

But equally A : D :: C : B = No Lemma.

This leads to Categorical Deduction, but it also suggests a mathematical problem of a double-horned dilemma about qualifiers.

As soon as lemmas are involved again, we get statements like:

A : A* :: B : B* which simply means that A : B :: A* : B*.

And, ultimately it ends up again at statements like:

A : B* :: C : D* which fit neatly into categorical deduction.

However, the neat 1 : 1 relationship is not always present in these more advanced comparisons.

Part II. The Third Sense: Infinite Extension

A theory that goes beyond these mathematical models of lemmas may be had with functional theories, yielding infinitely extended functions. Such a function is typically complex.

One word that could be used is 'interpretation', as in:

"Interpretation, interpretation*, interpretation**,

interpretation***, interpretation****...

interpretation*****, interpretation******..."

If the first interpretation is treated as itself a lemma (as in 0-d-equivalence-to-unity category theory), then this already extends to seven lemmas!

They can be interpreted as follows, in a complex view of formal category theory:

interpretation*: The formal qualification of a system. 'Strategy'.

interpretation**: The exceptions, empirical or other-wise, upon the system. 'Techniques'.

interpretation***: The secondary formal existence of the system, i.e. its systematic translation. 'Thoughts'.

interpretation****: The emergent applications of the system, e.g. to empirical reality. 'Tools'.

interpretation*****: The entities or real objects of the system. 'Truth'.

interpretation******: The meaning or higher significance of the objects of the system, such as laws, principles, or cultured facts. 'Strength'.

interpretation*******: The meaningful cultured environment of objects interacting meaningfully. 'Beauty'.

FORMAL / LOGICAL SYSTEMS

META-MATHEMATICS

One conception of meta-mathematics is the
'traditional' one, which says

that meta-mathematics is simply critical theory
about mathematics. In my

view, that usage belongs either to philosophy of
mathematics, or to

mathematics itself.

In my own usage, meta-mathematics is particularly
the formal extension

of mathematics through mathematical OR philosophical theories, derived

from the word 'meta-' meaning after.

Formalism has always had the reputation of being
metaphysical, and it is

no less the case in meta-mathematics (under my
definition).

Systems Theory

Here are four areas to study, to pique your interest in my definition of

Meta-Mathematics.

1. Category Theory[+], an extension of set theory. This is related to

modules, which are effectively relativistic versions of set groupings. A

key feature of category theory in my view is a system I invented called

coherent Categorical Deduction. This form of analogous to / replaces the

plus symbol from mathematics.

2. Paradoxical Formalism [-]. Paradox theory is a way of relating the

ultimate bounds of knowledge in a formalized way. Paradox is analogous

to the original, unconscious meaning of levels of analysis. Level 1 of

paradox is analogous to / replaces the minus symbol, and typically is

represented with potential dualities. At the level of duality, these are

solvable with categorical deduction. Otherwise,

they are solved with

paroxysm, which creates level 2. In level 2 [=], the Paroxysmic Method

is introduced, solving the paradox. Level 2 in my theory of Paradoxical

Formalism is analogous to / replaces the equals sign symbol or absolute

conditioning, by creating commutative levels of equivalency. Level 3 if

there is one [represented by three horizontal lines] might deal with

Synergies or Synergasms.

3. Judgment Theory [X]. This set of theories has to do with formal

iteration and consolidation of sets. For most pur-poses it is already

covered by Category Theory and Paradoxical For-malism. However, it is

an important teaching tool having to do with relative absoluteness, the

completeness of sets, and the incidents in which systems emerge

(typically in neutral, optimal, conditioned states). In my theory, Judgment theory is analogous to / replaces the multiplication sign, and can also be

interchangeable with theories of exponential growth, which relate with

theories of completeness and modularization.

4. Metalogical Theory [/]. Metalogical Theory is the extension of

category theory for non-closed sets, specifically infinite sets that exist

within a boundary. Proportional methods are used to yield relations

between parts of the internal set, or between the internal and the

external. As you might predict, in my theory, Meta-logical Theory is

analogous to / replaces the division sign in mathe-matics.

5. Entity Theory [{ } --> ||]. In addition, there is what might be called

entity theory, similar to judgment theory. Entity the-ory deals with the real

or theoretical status of symbols or other concepts as entities within the

system. This relates with such concepts as evaluation and parsing

processes, each of which serves the role of proving
a function for an

entity. Not only does proving in-terms-of-entity
seem necessary, but this

type of approach is also preferable because of its
capacity to define

systems elements on-the-fly. Thus, it is analogous
to / replaces proof

theory from mathematics.

FORMAL SYSTEMS

LOGICAL METHODOLOGY

In general, the logic is developed through a precise method, whether it is categorical, mathematical, or some other general system:

(1) Formulas, formal or informal.

(2) Variation, specific logics and methods.

(3) General Adaptation or quantification / universalizing, organizing: "putting it in its best form".

(4) Specialized Adaptations, suiting the system to a specific problem or discipline.

Considering this process, it becomes much easier to create logic.

FORMAL / LOGICAL SYSTEMS

CATEGORICAL DEDUCTIONS

{To my knowledge, categorical deductions were invented as a method of coherent knowledge as recently as 2013. I, Nathan Coppedge, was the inventor. It is an offshoot of an earlier project called The Unity Project that adopted an analogical format and also the characteristic Cartesianism. That two-part aspect is perhaps the most unique part of the method, although its implications are actually much more broad and important, as it provides a basis for true objectivity}.

Purpose: Categorical deductions are designed to yield objective knowledge on a wide variety of subjects.

How it works: Opposites are assumed to be exclusive of all territory between them. Opposites oppose along thediagonal, for example, in quadratics A opposes C, not B

or D. B opposes D, not C or A.

It may be though of as exponentially efficient, since four categories produces only two deductions.

The deductions are AB:CD and AD:CB strictly for quadra.

Systems Theory

The diagram looks like the following:

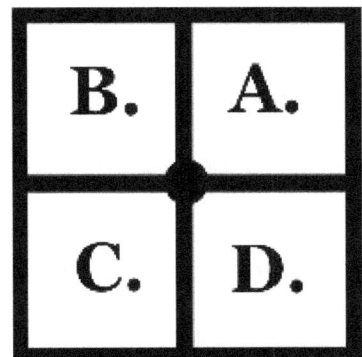

EXAMPLES

1. Paradox opposes non-paradox.

   wealth opposes poverty.

Deduction 1

"Wealth is paradoxical, then when it is empover-
ished it is un-paradoxical."

Deduction 2

"Wealth is un-paradoxical, then when it is impover-
ished it is paradoxical."

Other less obvious deductions are also possible:

2. Subjectivity opposes objectivity.

Determination opposes free-will.

Deduction 1

"Subjective determination objectifies the will."

Deduction 2

"Subjective will objects to (objective) determinism."

Categorical deductions can also be made with longer individual

category terms involving multiple words, with the assumption that

the exclusion concerns the coherent relevance of category A. If a

different category is seen as primary, a different context may

result. However, since the opposite of category A is pre-

determined, and it doesn't matter whether B or D is compared

first, then there is no effect on the system by the arbitrary choice.

Systems Theory

Further explanations of some of the details may be found on

Quora HERE.

There is also some similarity to the methods of Paroxysm (solution to all paradoxes, which operates in sets of neighboring categories compared to their opposites) and AOLT-THERE (which instead involves selecting a term AND an opposite within each category-square).

FORMAL / LOGICAL SYSTEMS

METHODS FOR SOLVING ALL PARADOXES

METHOD 1: PAROXYSM

A paroxysm or solution to all paradoxes may be found by

taking the opposite of EVERY term in the best definition

of the problem, in the same order as the original words.

METHOD 2: REVERSAL

When the problem must remain a paradox, reversal may still be
permitted. This might be called 'prodoxysm' (defined to mean
any problem that solves a problem). For example, the opposite
of problem AB is problem BA.

METHOD 3: UNIVERSALS

Adding universals may sometimes serve as a solution, because

they exist both within the problem, and within the solution, and thus, they remain valid throughout.

METHOD 4: GOD VARIABLES

Adding certain types of variables, such as those equivalent to an equals sign can result in solutions in terms of other such signs.

EXAMPLES OF METHOD 1: PAROXYSM

Sorites Paradox (Sound of Straw Falling):

Problem = Definite Continuum

Solution = Indefinite Definitions

Problem = Meaningless Continuum

Solution = Meaningful Divisions

Liar Paradox:

Problem = "Noun lies. I am a noun"

Solution = "Anti-noun does not lie. I am not a noun"

Problem = "I am nothing lying"

Solution = "Nothing lies absolutely".

Problem = "Nothing lies about the truth".

Solution = "Even liars can tell true lies".

Paradox of the Arrow:

Problem = "Infinite Divisions of Matter"

Solution = "Finite Continuity Concept"

(otherwise, time is infinite).

Balding Man:

"Involves ambiguity between hair and balding. The solution is

unambiguous hair and balding, or in other words, small amounts of hair or large amounts of covered scalp." (---The Dimensional

Philosopher's Toolkit, 3rd Ed. p. 187)

Examples from Metaphysics:

Some metaphysical paradoxes are not true paradoxes, meaning

that they are not as well suited as Zeno's paradoxes.

Nonetheless, insofar as they are paradoxes, solutions can be

attempted.

The Problem of the Brain-in-the-Vat is particularly difficult.

However, if it is seen as a metaphysical problem, then it has a

material solution. If it is seen as a physical problem, then it has
a

metaphysical solution. Otherwise it can be seen as a semantic

problem, which has a rhetorical solution (if it's a rhetorical

problem, however, it has a practical solution).

Metaphysical Paradox Described by Vlastos

"Ambiguous Middle Subject Problem"

"Arbitrary Extreme Context Solution"

Insisting it is a problem is insisting it has a solution.

Otherwise, it might not be a problem.

Or, it might not be universal.

EXAMPLES OF METHOD 2: REVERSAL

For example, 'having a paradox' might be a 'paradox of having'.

Having might not be a problem, or a paradox might not be a

problem.

'God's paradox' might be 'a paradoxical God'. Being without God

might be a solution.

A 'substantial paradox' might be a 'paradoxical substance'. Being

without substance could be a solution.

These use what are called syntactical opposites such as those

used in categorical deduction. A categorical deduction has a

formally identical syntactical opposite, as it's formal properties

are double-double-negativity.

EXAMPLES OF METHOD 3: UNIVERSALS

This may also be seen as a strong-arm version of prodoxysm, or

the solution by acceptability of the paradox.

For example, 'I love the paradox as it truly is' may be a solution

so long as love is universal, or so long as the paradox has

relevance.

Another example is if 'The paradox is functional just as it is'.

There might be an exceptional case where the paradox solves

more problems than it creates, in spite of being paradoxical.
For example, something similar to Solomon and the Baby. The
formal properties of this idea involve adding additional paradoxes to create a solution.

EXAMPLES OF METHOD 4: GOD VARIABLES

For example,

If a given paradox can be negated, this may create God in the

solution, if God is the opposite of nothing. Therefore, if one can

argue there is God, one might argue there is no paradox. Or,
one can argue that God is paradoxical, and therefore, there is
no problem with the paradox, since it is God. In my terminology
God is a variable that is the opposite of nothingness, and has
miraculous properties like being the sum of infinite undefined
variables.

Similarly, if the problem is 'one' the solution may be 'infinite', if

infinity is the opposite of 'one'. Or, an infinite problem may have

just one solution. This principle is summed up by the idea of

exceptionality.

Systems Theory

By extension, the variables of coherence and incoherence can

also be used opposing each other. A problem involving incoherent

'nothing' would implicate a coherent god. The only way to create a problem here would be if the problem was universal, or if
god was incoherent, or if nothing was universal, or if the problem is absolute, or under exceptional conditions, approximately.

Some of the above is also available as an academic article with

citations at: THE SOLUTION TO ALL PARADOXES

FORMAL SYSTEMS

PRINCIP-PUZZLE

Principle-Puzzle or Princip-Puzzle is a rare logic drawn from the analogy that principle occupies one of any number of geometric categories.

So, for example, in a 2-d typology such as a bounded Cartesian Coordinate system similar to a truth-table, except exclusive, principle might occupy one of the four categories of a system (say, in generating proofs, for example). Think of principle as a kind of description of the necessity for logical ingredients.

Now, we can analogize that the presence of principle defines that

two categories within the same diagram can oppose principle, but

that one category can no more than cancel it out. Thus, we can

see that some sort of irrationality is required in 1/2 of the categories if we are to oppose the idea of having principle.

Incidentally, the 1/2 ratio (maximum) is precisely the point at

which reason becomes diametrically opposed to madness, thus

reducing the system to a pair of opposites and eliminating the

logic. Thus, principle becomes provably a figure of logic. And, at

the same time, we can see that when 1/2 is madness, principle

composes 1/2 of reason, thus, there still remains 1/2 of reason

which may be not yet defined. Thus, combining some further idea

with principle is what creates reason.

That's the full description of what Princip-Puzzle means for a 2-d

typology. Here is the diagram:

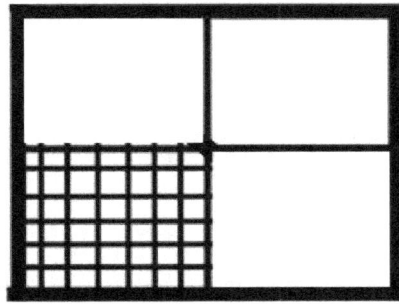

PRINCIP-PUZZLE 1 (2-D)

A second princip-puzzle which I hit upon recently inspired this

writing. It relates to analogizing between 4-d metaphysics and a

3-part typology. Once again, principle is one geometric category,

but in this case it is left unstated, and simply rounds out the

3-typology to make it adequate for 4-d metaphysics. In other

words, it is creating an application of 3-d categories that has a

principle of 4-d by having a 4th category that represents principle.

The 4-d construction is 3-d because it is a construction based
on

principles, and the variable called 'principles' already counts as

one dimension, when it is taken seriously (i.e. when it is

quantifiable like all typological categories theoretically are).

The three further categories I came up with are:

1. Root / origin: Identity.

2. Connector / conjunction: Balance.

Systems Theory

3. Structure / filler: Infinity.

Make sense? Here is the diagram in that order. Notice that the

nodes have different interpretations of what principle means, and

are fairly exclusive for the set.

PRINCIP-PUZZLE 2

(4-D METAPHYSICS)

FORMAL / LOGICAL SYSTEMS

THE VESSELEXT

A vesselext is a series of compartments in which each
compartment does some logical operation. The compartments are
typically arranged in a horizontal series, in which the size,
grouping, and angularity of the compartments communicates
something about their logical operation (In Chinese the
apartments might be arranged vertically...)

HOW TO MAKE A VESSELEXT

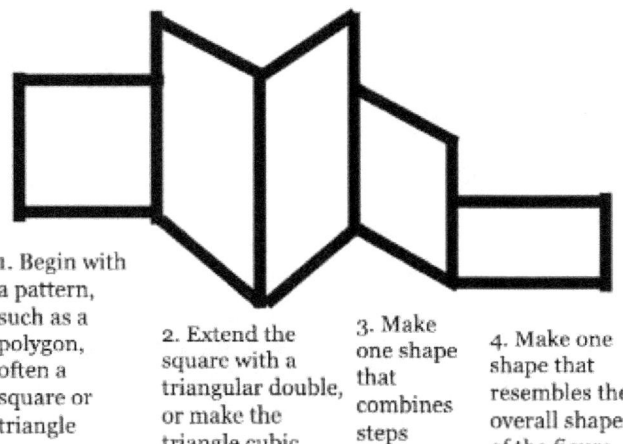

1. Begin with a pattern, such as a polygon, often a square or triangle

2. Extend the square with a triangular double, or make the triangle cubic and triple

3. Make one shape that combines steps 1 and 2

4. Make one shape that resembles the overall shape of the figure

Finally, Instructions: In step one, take a general concept. In step two provide two or three ideas on the subject. In step three, take the smallest part of the first idea, and all of the second, or part of the second if you have a third, and all of the third if you have a third. In step four, apply the general concept to the concept from step three.

ADDITIONAL INSTRUCTIONS:

In step two, try to pick two or three expressions, preferably single

words, which collectively form a definition about the term from

step one. In step three, go through an initial process of what it

means to have more of the later parts than the earlier parts.

Actually do some thinking. Then formulate the best expression that briefly expresses all of the best knowledge on that subject,

using those words, and very few others, or else, by a rational

deduction from one part being greater or 'all', and the other being

smaller or 'necessary'. In step four, use thinking in a more cas-
ual

way, attempting to find the most interesting combination of step

three and step one. The result should ideally be clever, or simply

very true, and the vesselext is designed to give those kinds of

results, but it depends on the perfection of the previous steps.

EXAMPLES OF THE VESSELEXT

1. war. 2. yin and yang 3. mastery, 4. mastery of war

1. Science. 2.not art, not bad. 3. Good, bad art. 4. There is a

science to bad art.

1. Logical, 2. Synthetic, Rational 3. Rationalized reality 4. Logic

is rationalized.

Systems Theory

1. Errors. 2. Time and Place. 3. Clockwork 4. Wrong time.

1. Ideas. 2. Reality and Imagination. 3. Reality is worth it.

4. Ideas are worth it.

1. Language. 2. Eloquence and Knowledge. 3. Knowledge of

eloquence 4. Knowledge is an eloquent language

1. Virtue. 2. Bonificence and Pragmatism. 3. Striving. 4. Strive
for

virtue.

1. Aesthetics. 2. Complexity, Perfection. 3. There is potential for

perfection. 4. Art has the potential for perfection.

1. Variable. 2. Value, Property. 3. All properties have value.

4. All properties of variables have value.

1. Criticism. 2. Theory, Generation.3. Theory is about generation.

4. Theories of criticism are about generation.

1. Creativity. 2. Energy, Ideas. 3. All ideas involve energy.

4. All ideas involve creative energy.

1. Metaphysics. 2. Paths & Levels. 3. Every level has a path.

4. Every metaphysical level has a path.

1. Priority. 2. Standard, Approximity. 3. Standard at length.

4. At length, standards are a priority.

1. Legend. 2. Myth and Magic. 3. Potency has a little truth.

4. Potent truths are somewhat legendary.

1. Garage. 2. Car Housing. 3. We have it covered. 4. A garage can fit more than one car.

1. Determinism. 2. Free will and Fate. 3. The fates have a will.

4. The fates have a determined will.

Systems Theory

1. Architecture. 2. Design, Construction. 3. Everything has a plan.

4. Everything in architecture has a plan.

1. Process. 2. Dynamic Function. 3. Perfect energy. 4. Processes

perfect energy.

These may have been the only Vesselexts ever created!

FORMAL / LOGICAL SYSTEMS

AOLT-There

Affecting Objective Language Translation, Theory-Has-it-

Everything-Reverses-Everything (A.O.L.T. - T.H.E.R.E.)

General Diagram:

SIMPLE METHOD

Take four statements and place them in each of four boxes.
Write

the opposite within any two neighboring boxes, then read the unchanged terms and the opposite terms in any cyclical order, inputting any helpful non-negating connectives. In an advanced form, the connectives may even include expressions such as 'knowledge of' / 'about' or 'helpful with'. In all, there are four different combinations for any four terms. To help with formulating these, it may be helpful to write both the original term

and the opposite within each box.

EXAMPLES

For Freedom Fighter Political War

We write:

[1] Freedom / Prison

[2] Fighter / Peaceful

[3] Political / No opinion

[4] War / Peace

Outputs look something like the following:

Pacifist Freedom: War of No Opinions

Political War: Peaceful Prison

War of Peace: No Opinion About Freedom

And,

Prison of Peace, Political Fighter

Now let's choose a second context to study.

For Thoughts About Impending War

We write:

[1] Thoughts / Stupidity

[2] About / Nonsense

[3] Impending / Distant

[4] War / Peace

Systems Theory

The output looks like the following:

About thoughts: peaceful distance /

Stupid nonsense: impending war /

Thoughts of war: distant nonsense /

Peaceful stupidity: about the impending.

Now let's find a third context to study.

For Multiple Worlds Free Will

We write:

[1] Multiple / Singular

[2] Worlds / Nothing

[3] Free / Determined

[4] Will / When?

The output looks like this:

Worlds multiply when determined /

Simple wills liberate nothing /

Nothing singular wills liberation /

Nothing multiplies the will to be determined.

These cases may be sufficient evidence to prove the method has

some value, even if it is on the disjunctive side.

FORMAL / LOGICAL SYSTEMS

EXCEPTIONISM

A general introduction might be with the concept of an 'afocal network'. Which is a network in which the progression organizes disrelations. For example, [Set 1] might be oriented towards the idea that everything is an original, undifferentiated experience. Perfect, but amoral. [Set 2] might differ in two major characteristics: it might be oriented towards the idea that 'we don't want to be midgets, and that's the bottom line!' imperfect but ethical. [Set 3] Might be making artwork from dead leaves: neither ethical nor unethical, neither moral nor immoral.

Exceptionism is generally the logic of limits upon a system, the way of finding extensions to an existing system. Ideally exceptions are formulated so as to be 'accessible' which is terminology borrowed from Graph Theory meaning that as many possible applied theories benefit from the general categories of exception such that the general categories of exception manifest

the greatest possible, the most universal, relevance for all applied theories.

Here are some exceptional rules of exception:

Something is part of everything, if there is anything in everything.

Everything is at least one thing.

We can make everything that we can make everything of.

Nothing is the only nothing, unless it is plural and the same.

Another way of stating the concept of exceptions is in terms of clauses, or what is called clausality. This is simply a way of measuring the number of assumptions necessary to reach a given law or proposition. In general, however, the smallest number of premises is necessary to reach ideal laws. Therefore, general (philosophical) exceptionism as opposed to applied exceptionism tends to deal with clauses in terms of their universal relevance, and only deems them appropriate if they are unimpeachable, which can mean that to the extent they are trivial, they are wrong.

So, here is another axiom:

To the extent that they are trivial, they are wrong

[Meta-Exceptionism]

Systems Theory

FORMAL / LOGICAL SYSTEMS

AMETAPH

A-Metaphorical System:

Level 1: Structural Ametaph

Structural ametaph is simply continuousness expressed as

discontinuousness. This can be analogized to a grid in which each

line-segment of each square is a different color. The overall

structure depends on having infinite colors that are equally

well-expressed. The finite structure simply depends on the logical

relationship of the discontinuities.

Level 2: Structure Vs. Metaphor

The clear exception to structural ametaph is metaphor, since

ametaph means a-metaphorical. Either metaphor breaks down

into structural non-metaphor, which results in structural

ametaph,or metaphor breaks down in a non-structural way. Here

we get the second level.

Ironically, in terms of structural ametaph, astructural ametaph

expresses itself as a metaphorical structure, by accounting for all

the negatives in the expression astructural ametaph, we get

structural metaphor.

However, at the same time, in at least one degree it must be

neither metaphorical nor structural. So, the clearest

representation of Level 2 may be 'one degree of de-structural

literalism'. If we treat level 2 as metaphorical structure, this

earlier insight leads to level 3.

Level 3: Literalism Vs. Structure Vs. Metaphor

Ametaph level 3 concerns finding a de-structural relationship

expressed in terms of continuity between metaphor: structure:

literalism. One approach is to take a symbol (literalism)

arbitrarily related to a system (metaphor), arbitrarily related to

an interpretation (structure), and then interpret what is

discontinuous between these things as a way of binding system to

structure (continuity).

EXAMPLES: OF AMETAPH

Structure: Infinite Variation.

Structural Metaphor: Differentiation, Epiphany, Journey

Literal Metaphor Structure:

1. A tree (symbol) is the world (system) when it has importance to

the world (interpretation), when it grows on the world (symbolic

interpretation), and the world grows similar to the tree by having

a tree grow on it (systemic interpretation).

2. The letter 'O' (symbol) is an organ (system) when 'organ'

begins with 'O' (interpretation) and when 'O' is the first letter of

organ, organ is a symbol represented by 'O' (symbolic

interpretation). And when 'organ' is a symbol, it can be

represented by 'O' (systemic interpretation).

3. A man (system) does something with his hand (symbol),

because a man has a hand (symbolic interpretation), and a
man

does everything a man can do (systemic interpretation). Thus,
a

man does something with a hand (interpretation).

The foregoing provides a general and circumspect guide on this

'new' discipline, which might in fact date to ancient Egypt,

judging by the name.

Systems Theory

FORMAL / LOGICAL SYSTEMS

QUALIFICS

Qualifics is the science of qualities. In this sense, it adopts the formality of science, along with the so-called "soft side" of psychology. However, it owes its motivation to philosophy, which conveniently tends to be seen between those two areas.

The important thing about qualifics is that it deals with qualities.

The earliest qualific science was simply philosophizing about essence. Since then, science, logic, and mathematics have offered tools for interpreting essence or qualia critically, , for example, by correlating length with intensity.

However, since qualifics always deals with qualities, what we mean by criticism is really criticism qua essence.

That is the second beginning-point for qualifics.

The next beginning-point is 'how to fill in criticism such that
criticism has qualities?' It is the answer to this question
that defines a given qualific theory.

In fact, it is even possible to arbitrarily decide that the area of
concern is not criticism at all, but something else formal.
However, this secondary approach implies a formal lens, and a
system of exceptions related through the adopted tools to the
original case of 'something filling criticism'. In this way,
qualifics is related to theories of formal exceptions.

Next, we enter 'Intermediate Qualifics' which is the theory
of how to define the formalism such that it has qualities.
At this point it bears some resemblance to the Greek
theories of the physiologos, or early metaphysical thinkers,
except that these theories being defined aren't necessarily
theories about an entire world. Instead, they may define

exceptionally useful approaches to logic, language, or other critical tools for interpreting the world.

Through criticism, qualities are granted a capacity to claim a territory of experience.

At this point, which is still Intermediate, a philosophical and linguistic concept called Mereology can be introduced. This is the concept of treating objects on their own terms. It also implies treating objective interpretations as objects qua interpretation. What this means is that all factors being considered in a perspective have a say in how the perspective is critiqued and rendered.

Extending Intermediate Qualifics, mereology leads to the use of critical lenses which are the first major logical tool of qualifics. A critical lens in this case is simply a rule about the impression and organization of the qualified object.

These rules may often take the form of quantification of a critical

terminology, or else a position of infinite regress, either of which

represents the organization of all the represented qualia.

For example, qualifics may take terms like 'system', 'bromide',

'esthetic thesis', and 'variable' and reach statements such as the

following, which qualify something about the organization of the

impression (These 'organizations of impressions' are often

qualified in some way, hence the name 'qualifics'):

*Traveling System ("All systems travel" ||standard||)

*Bromide Changes ("Functions change, bromides change,

    bromide must be that which changes")

*Esthetic Theses are Contexts ("Theses are touches")

*Variables must be Highly Qualified (||Qualia variables||).

At an advanced level of qualifics, terminology such as emerges

from Intermediate Qualifics are thrown around as standard tools

of qualification and criticism, returning and reiterating the idea of

a critical lens, and informing aesthetic choices as well as

rhetorical arguments.

VARIATIONS ON QUALIFICS

Qualific Darwinism: This is a variation on Qualifics in which

excesses of certain qualities lead to death. The condition of
dying

from such qualities is termed 'overexposure'. A critical element
of

overexposure is that multiple qualities of different types have

been combined. It is the complex negativity and terminal

perfection that leads to death. Another way to describe it is that

death is being efficient or cheap. Thus, the things that survive
in

Qualific Darwinism tend to be inefficient, expensive things. A

translation of this, however, is that it includes efficient biological

processes. Biology is efficient, but not fatally efficient.

FORMAL / LOGICAL SYSTEMS

ENTICS

Entics, the science of entities, otherwise known as the entic science, is a discipline that has a long history, but is rarely named as such. It is viciously divided between an empirical approach (biology, physics, etc.) and metaphysical philosophy (ontology, how things exist).

I.

Entics may be described initially in terms of an item, and the datum in which the item is understood.

Depending on the manner in which entities are interpreted, the

datum may take the form of mathematical dimensions, a context of interaction (such as intelligent networks), or a logical

relationship such as a philosophical system or linguistic pattern.

II.

Ideally, entities (items) have some kind of significance in terms of

the formal context in which the item is being interpreted. A common result is to find that the item falls into the following classifications:

1: Trivial (not affecting the context at all).

2: Un-exceptional (not affecting the context meaningfully).

3: Typical (affecting the context in a normal way).

Additionally, some items may in some cases be (0:) completely meaningless (be careful with this by using absolute criteria), but otherwise if they don't fit into the above, they fall into the following more advanced categories:

4. Functional (following a predictable pattern).

5. Organized (having a particular effect).

6. Exceptional (following a characteristic pattern).

7. Unique (having a highly notable effect or pattern).

8. Game-changing (changing the way the datum behaves)

As can be seen, this initial type of analysis results in ranking items in terms of their uniqueness, with the assumption that unique internal logic defines unique external logic.

III.

Next, at a more advanced level we have relations of multiple

objects (symbols) or items (entities), and we wish to find common significance amongst them.

This can be done through the following properties:

1. Existence (Yes / No).

2. Commonality (Degree / Characterization)

3. Oppositeness (Opposition / Exclusion)

4. Modal Similarities (Opposed but similar?

   Basically similar or basically different?)

5. Unique Attributes (Common and different classifications)

Readers may note the similarity to principles from syllogisms,

such as existence and exclusion.

This process serves to classify in exactly which ways, vis. the earlier categories, these items, objects or entities express

exterior attributes.

IV.

An important tool in entics is the concept of 'digging' which is an

additional extension of analysis which asks us to get the most out of any one concept. Effectively, the only limitation on digging is normativity which defines that a previous object is already significant.

Thus, a first rule of entics is that items tend to be significant. This is because the only possibility of finding significance for an object is finding some way in which it has significant for other objects which are already significant. Thus, an object has to be

doubly-significant to have special significance. Simply relating

with one significant object is not enough, and relating with two

objects may require some form of logic.

A second rule is that items express interior logic through

relevance, or else through experience.

Thus, some of the broadest possible categories of relevance

and

experience might be helpful:

Relevance Experience:

1. Appearance.

2. Influence.

3. Symbolism.

4. Scintillation.

Experience:

1. Notion.

2. Representation.

3. Excitation.

4. Awareness.

Thus we get the primary logic for internal entities through the following:

{(Appearance & Influence & Symbolism & Scintillation)

V

Systems Theory

(Notion & Representation & Excitation & Awareness)}

Thus, relevance and experience are fundamentally based on causes (scintillations, etc.) and origins (notions, etc.).

Thus, an entity may be explained generally as a causal origin.

V. (The role of Quantification).

In some cases a system exists exclusively through quantification, and it is quantification that expresses the existence of system.

This is true for example, with simplified concepts of evolution or Moore's Law of Computing (that technology quadruples its complexity every six months, or something like that).

In these cases, the entity (such as technology) represented by the system (such as technological growth) amounts to a power difference. Thus, the system amounts to a number such as 2, 3 or 4 which represents an exponent on a field of data.

Most other differences expressed in these terms are variations within pre-existing data, such as can be accommodated by adding or subtracting large numbers from the equation's data set. For example, with anthropological data about someone's age, we might predict longer potential age the longer someone succeeds to survive. So, actual age can be approximated as an extended

tail with a probability of (1 / sq root of n) + (1 / the average life expectancy in years), where n is the number of years lived.

FORMAL / LOGICAL SYSTEMS

IRRATIONAL LOGIC

At some point in examining the tables of categories, one might observe a singular problem: the problem of simultaneous differences, or in other words, paradoxical naive realism.

As an example, consider that on the one hand we have:

"Knowing of Pain"

This can be translated to mean essentially that pain is bad, and perhaps the desire for pleasure or something more meaningful or substantial than pain, such as Meaning or The Ultimate.

On the other hand, what if pain gives life reality, and when pain is missing, we miss the Real Dimension of life? In that case, we get a second concept, which is:

"Knowing FROM Pain"

However, the two concepts are incompatible, because they arise for vastly different reasons. In the first case ("of"), pain arises in excessive proportions, whereas in the second case ("from"), pain arises as a special signifier of reality that once existed.

One can observe this difference for example in the 'hostage

syndrome' and Pavlov's dogs.

How does this show that irrationality is a system? Well, if we take the case as exemplary of the most objective emotions, that is, those that are purely symbolic and may be given or taken, this serves to exemplify at least one degree of universal irrationality.

This is supported by the understanding that conventional definitions of pleasure and pain are suited to naive realism or else objective knowledge----that is, relativism or else prescriptivism.

So far as irrationality is concerned, categorical knowlege is similar to naive realism: both accept either a category or a relation of categories as the basis for knowledge. But irrationality rejects the obviousness of categories and also relations of categories. It has a less obvious structure.

Let me elaborate what I know from the 'FROM' relationship.

1. Irrationality can be a vector.

2. The vector can carry further content, which may or may not be

irrational.

3. The irrational treats rational and irrational content the same

way.

4. The irrationality of the vector is conserved.

Thus, in simple terms, irrationality involves adding the qualification that something is 'irrational'. At first, one might suppose that either irrationality is a rational assessment of an irrational condition, whose vector is judgment, or irrationality is an irrational assessment of a condition which cannot be deemed rational because of a lack of judgment.

However, irrational judgments may be possible, and this is the only real way to qualify irrationality for logic. If what we mean by judgment is a lack of standards, then there is no formal irrational logic. So, what we mean by irrational logic entails irrational standards or an irrational context.

The best way to guarantee irrational logic at this point is to grant that an irrational context provides a means for granting irrational standards. But at this point, irrationality is no different from categorical logic in that respect. And, it seems to simply involve a 'freer' form of rationality, that is, one without limits on its standards. But, nonetheless, there appears to be a limit, conceptually. For it may be determined that irrationality must have a context or a vector of irrationality. If there were no vector, then a context would be required, much as a lack of deductive argument implies empiricism.

Thus, there may be four types of irrational arguments:

1. Vector

This is simply a qualifier that something is irrational. It may or may not be proven that the thing actually is irrational. In other words, it is conditional. What is irrational is that it is unknown whether the thing is, could be, or under some definition is, irrational. This is also called relative irrationality. If everything were irrational, the concept of nothing would be relatively rational. At this point what is irrational is that rationality has a standard. However, it is still possible for irrationality to meet the standard of reasonableness, through paradox.

2. Context

This is also called qualified irrationality. It is the check against total irrationality. It is something that seems irrational even if it isn't. It is irrational under some definition. Systems of this type might include naive realism, paradoxes, or incoherency. Problems are created to solve, so it is neither irrational nor rational. But it is not yet meaningless. It has semantic content in a condition of suspense. Rational numbers for example, might be fancifully irrational in this way, because they can be multiplied by i.

3. Double-negation

This type produces meaninglessness. It is a form of existential failure. It may involve making demands on reason. It might exist

this way under absolute definitions. This amounts to complexity exclusively, across the board, thus leading to universal irrationality. It may remain irrational after it is defined (for example, the notorious undefined functions).

4. Excessive rationality

Concepts, in particular like (A) Stupidity*, (B) Over-complexity, (C) Genius, and (D) Under-complexity have this type of character. They are more complex than they appear at first, at least if viewed as forms of irrationality. This is explained by an imbalance between the tools used to perceive and the perceptionitself. Irrational semantics is created, which in turn provides a basis for infinite irrationality as an extension of reason.

*The concept of stupidity is similar to contingency, in that alternate systems can be swapped in without regard for rules. The rule tends to be that stupidity is in proportion to genius, but not vice versa. In other words, genius borrows from stupidity or it doesn't, and otherwise it's about complexity. These types of correlations become a relatively solid basis for general concepts of irrationality.

Systems Theory

FORMAL / LOGICAL SYSTEMS

PROBLEMATICS

In terms of 3-d, 1-d Problems are solved through finding relevance.

In terms of 3-d, 2-d Problems are solved by discovering what the matter is.

3-d problems are solved by finding priority. Beauty is one possible solution. But, functionality is better. Intelligence is better than functionality. And, happiness is better than intelligence. In this way, a philosophical structure is created. Wisdom is found through ugliness, shortcuts, gifts, and knowledge.

'Survival is a mode of existence. This means that we survive.' The essence of this formula is only realized in the 4th dimension, because the fourth dimension is where recursive time is permitted. Problems still exist in the 4th dimension, but in terms of the 3rd dimension they are 'eternal' problems, rather than stupid ones.

FORMAL / LOGICAL SYSTEMS

ELIDIAN LEAPS

An Elidian leap involves moving to a new, equal, ideal category of thought. The many angles at which the concept must be approached make it challenging. In many cases, the leap requires a new vocabulary, such as with eteration = contingent iteration. One must not only think outside the box, but also understand exactly what definition would qualify to organize the new concept.

'H' Type. This is a standard parallel category type, analogous to modular extension. For example, 'World 2'.

'N' Type. In this case the second category is further-off. Some additional term such as 'archaic' or 'modern' has been applied to it to fit it to its new role. It is no longer organized in relation to the original concept except through multiple types of variation. This type is useful for specific applications. For example, 'Metaphor'.

'S' Type. In this case the concept differs only by lemma (quantity), and therefore the collective categories may be seen as singular, folded, and overlapping. A single variable defines the modular extension, and the form or orientation of the category rather than its position may define its role. For example, 'Evolution'.

Systems Theory

FORMAL / LOGICAL SYSTEMS

GENIUS

Alpha 'Waves': Learn calculus.

Beta: About business. There are many kinds of business.

Gamma: Choose a religion.

Delta: Learn to use delta.

Eta: Do things fast.

Zeta: Learn about drugs.

Epsilon: Control your urges.

Theta: Gain knowledge.

Iota: Demonstrate perfection.

Kappa: Explore politics.

Lambda: Ambitiously extend your activity.

Mu: Learn how to die.

Nu: Learn how to collect intelligence.

Omicron: Learn advanced studies.

Pi: Re-learn everything you've learned, only better.

Rho: Become a legend.

Sigma: Become a doctor.

Tau: Become unique.

Upsilon: Rule the world.

Phi: Teach.

Chi: Make deals.

Psi: Think.

Intermediate: Applications.

Omega: Pleasure, and say goodbye.

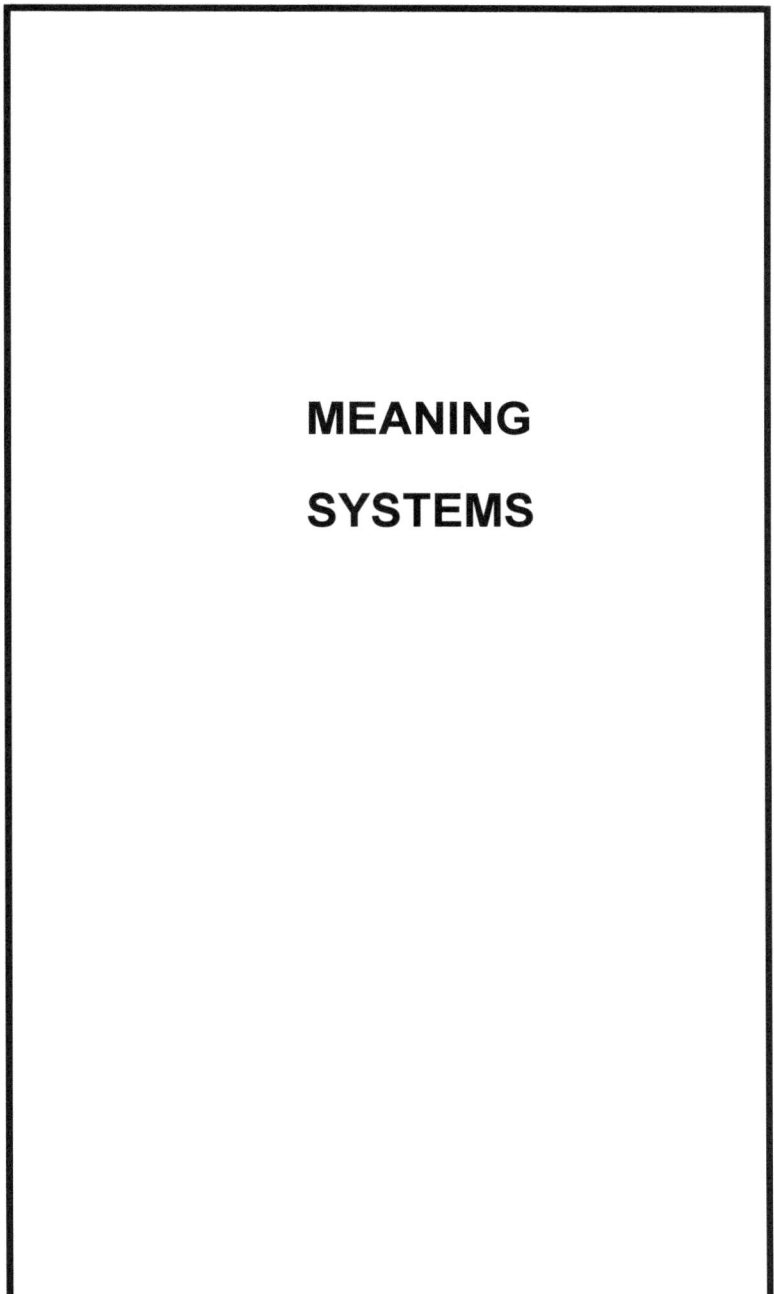

MEANING

SYSTEMS

Nathan Coppedge

MEANING SYSTEMS

AFFIRMATIVISM

For each thing, know that it is good for something. If the something is not good, it can be avoided. What is left is a world of good things.

Now ask, what is the best arrangement of these things? When the best arrangement is found, we have found the Affirmative World. The affirmative world is a world in which everything is good.

We can ask, does an ethical belief originate from an Affirmative World? Then many virtues amount to reaching the good world, whether it is psychological or physical, whether it is admitted or not admitted.

If it does not originate in Affirmation, it must be practical to be a true virtue.

MEANING SYSTEMS

AUTHENTICITY

We can seek what is good and authentic about each thing, such as a sweet, crisp Bosc pear, or an intellectual news gazette. There is an Epicurean element to appreciating nearly everything. Nearly everything has some special quality, either aesthetically, or in the abstract.

Each thing has harmony with everything else. Each thing has a certain resonance or justice within the larger scheme of things.

Now we select just the right things, with the right attitude, from amidst everything, and we begin to feel as if we belong in everything, as if our habit of being is in tune with everything. We can find loyal symbols of this process: things of significance, that make it easier to return to the state of belongingness. Languages and sciences can be formed of the most familiar and the most fascinating things, and lead us on ever deeper quests of self-searching and manifest permanence. If things disappear, if things lack value, it is because somehow we have not found meaning. Therefore, in this way, we can perceive the justice of life on the basis of meaning. And, it all goes back to the fundamental bases of experience, like the Bosc pear.

MEANING SYSTEMS

ABRIDGEMENT

At one of the greatest scales of abridgement the technique Is to render the original material ersatz, creating complexity. Next, there is the theory of translation or interpretation, creating doubles which do not literally complexify everything. Next, it may be possible to keep or refurbish the original text similar to how it already was presented. Then, there are ways to find a synopsis of the text to abbreviate its significance. A synopsis may be close to the same length, like a translation, or take the form of an abstract that serves the purpose of explaining the function and content of the material. Finally, there is a technique of using 'souls' and perhaps keeping only the souls, or only the most essential information, like a bulleted list. Next, there may be a way to capture just the title, or just information by one index or another, rather than a complete description.

MEANING SYSTEMS

ANYTHING THEORY*

Anything can be wonderful, if we know that anything is wonderful.

Now, what if there is no qualification for knowing. What if 'wonderful' is how anything is?

Doesn't it require proof to deny this principle, once it is declared subjective? Aren't we free to find 'wonderful' in anything?

Apparently, there is nothing that denies that a theory is wonderful, and thus, there is nothing that denies that we, and our thoughts, are wonderful!

The wonderful is no more than the qualification that everything is wonderful. And it is much less likely that nothing is wonderful. Categorically, however, only wonderful things are wonderful, but if something is wonderful, then everything about it is in some way wonderful!

*Inspired by Calculus.

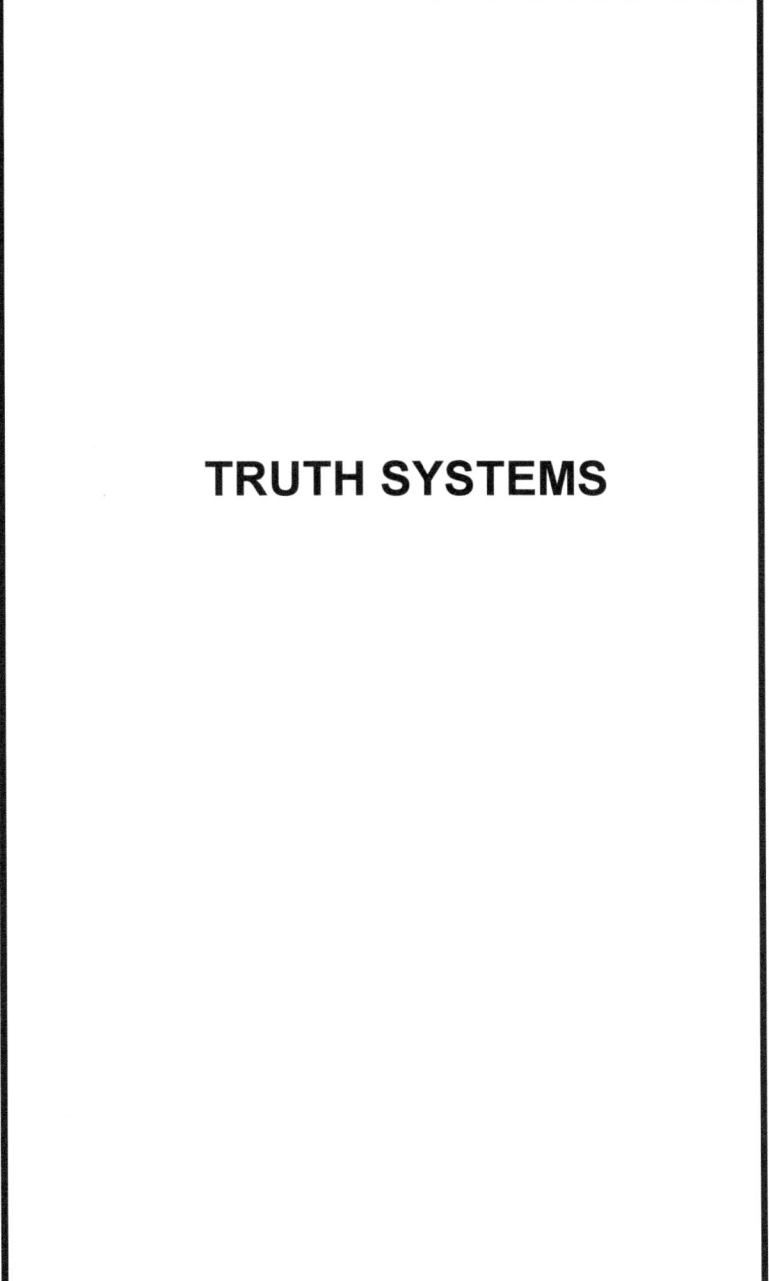

TRUTH SYSTEMS

TRUTH SYSTEMS

VERIDICATION

The method for finding proven truths.

Existing method: Form an exclusion and justify / defend some aspect of the exclusion. Then select amongst the parts to determine what is justified and not justified, or if both sides are justified, then in what way each is justified in terms of opposite particulars.

Un-existing method: Determine what does not exist yet and form an exclusion with what already exists in terms of opposites. Then, choose exclusive parts, either divided into purely new and purely old, or instead each divided equally between the new and the old, and in either case make one the alternative to the other.

See Also: Categorical Deduction.

TRUTH SYSTEMS

BRAID OF CORRESPONDENCES

(AMOUNTING TO A SPEED COURSE IN IMMORTAL-
ITY)

At the umpteenth degree of ordinary analysis, patterns emerge. One is left with riddles.

EXAMPLE 1 (MAJOR EXAMPLE):

One such riddle is found by calculating the soul of
the book titled

"The Elixir of Immortal Life".

The soul reads: "If you concoct a solution that was
not of

Mercury or Morgana what you can trust is not the
solution to the drug. " From this we can reach an
insight about Mercury and Morgana, which is the
first braid:

FIRST BRAID: Morgana is women in general, and
Mercury is the people missing! (people who have
died through the ages).

Systems Theory

From this we can reach a puzzle about Mercury and Morgana, which is the second braid:

BRAID 2: What if women are missing, and Mercury is a goddess

or a danger? From this we get the alchemical significance of this particular braid, which is that time is passing quickly and there is only one goddess. Women might help, but they are just as bad as Morgana. If one asks Mercury for help, she is a goddess traveling quickly like quicksilver.

If we want further meaning, we must translate further, accepting all truths that have already been explained.

BRAID 3: What if you have a daughter named Athena? If Athena is already present, then we can go on to another braid.

At this point 'braid' has been interpreted in a Motley way to mean 'bride'. However, Athena isn't necessarily important unless we want to know the meaning of quicksilver. That might be a distraction, since in the original soul of the Elixir of Life, Mercury was a problem, not a solution. We could look for a solution through Morgana, or we could continue the puzzle. Do we want someone named 'Brad'? Then that is a Motley solution that ends the braid. Otherwise, we continue...

BRAID 4: Do we want to be 'quick' or 'silver'? That might point towards Morgana the Goddess.

BRAID 5: Now the solutions concern either Quicksilver or the Goddess Morgana. Does the Goddess Morgana have the Elixir of Life? Can you become immortal by changing form? If the answer to these questions is no, then continue to the next braid. Otherwise, immortality may already have some practical solutions.

BRAID 6: Can you raise the dead, or become timeless? Then you have another type of practical solution.

BRAID 7:

Perhaps you can die forever, or war with the gods? If being alive is absolutely a war with the gods, these answers are both obvious, but there is a choice.

BRAID 8:

Can you transform Mercury into Gold, or kill time? Wisdom may be important for immortal life.

BRAID 9:

Can you make time golden, or bargain with time?

Negotiations may be important if you are not wise, and negotiations may end better if you are.

BRAID 10:

Can you make material payments or settle for less?

These are less fortunate answers, but may sometimes be valuable to appreciate. Appreciating your life may acquire value.

BRAID 11:

Can you become immaterial or unattached, or spend less time, or do something physically different?

These guesses may settle things that were not yet clear.

BRAID 12:

Can you give up the ghost, or is time insignificant, or you have a new soul, or you need to stop meditating, or you need to have sex, or you need to turn the hour glass?

These results might conclude the search for everyone, unless

some further combination is possible.

BRAID 13:

At this point Athena breaks down and takes drugs. The result is

Verdegris, which helps people with infinite ability to construct it.

However, for average people the biggest help might be a college degree, membership in the Golden Dawn, the Invisible Hand, the Illuminati, etc.

"Believe in yourself" appears to be Jesus' motto at this time.

The gods seem to be cruel.

The literal answers roughly amount to the idea that your new soul is immortal.

ADVANCED LEVEL

THE FOLDING OF THE BRAID

Now imagine that

(1: the first fold) the soul changes.

AND

(2: the second fold) the change can make one immortal.

Now it appears there is a road to immortality!

EXAMPLE 2: THE TWISTED BRAID (MINOR EXAMPLE)

You start with 'mild tea'.

Braid 1: Or is it 'the mild T'? Obscurity.

Braid 2: Or is it 'the mild TT?' At this point one might forget what tea means.

Braid 3: Or is it 'mild T.E.A.?' Such as 'to each another?' or 'technical employment association?'

Braid 4: Somehow one must know, it is not T, TT, or T.E.A. and thus it is tea!

Systems Theory

TRUTH SYSTEMS

PRESCRIPTIONS

In a high-minded concept of medicine, it is possible to

arrive at particular archetypal prescriptions.

Because they are so practical, I am putting them under 'Truth Systems'...

1. What looks like a problem, but is purely mental, is not really a problem.

2. What matters most is metaphysics.

3. The soul is the solution to any problem.

TRUTH SYSTEMS

ACQUISITION THEORY

There can be an ultimate truth.

For example,

"A sexual woman is a shlamazel

(someone who causes accidents"

The fact that the truth is ultimate does not mean that it is no where nearby.

In short, ultimate truths can be immediate truths.

Systems Theory

TRUTH SYSTEMS

METAPHYSICAL PERSPECTIVISM

Let us say that all perspectives, by some stretch of relation, belong to the same world, the same 'Venn-like compilation.' Now it is a matter of whether one concept absolutely blocks out the existence of another. Some concepts will belong in the same world, some concepts will be fictions, some concepts will be blocked out, and some concepts will be treated as imaginary, but will not be blocked out, much like Alexius Meinong's concept of a pile of money that never existed. Now, we can picture that each such concept in the world exists for some reason, because of some purpose, but each purpose may be somewhat obscure. Some purposes are obvious and explicable, and need no further purpose. Some purposes are complex enough to be explicable but not obvious, like calculus or a butterfly effect. Other purposes are neither obvious nor explicable, and some are obviously inexplicable, like an intentionally-confusing haiku. Depending on what it is, a thing may belong to any permutation of those two sets. For example, a haiku may be obscure, but understandable in our world because of the perverse psychology of the haikuist. Many concepts are explained by psychology or the lack thereof. In another case, some aspects of the world may exist because someone doesn't realize that they are perversely inspired ideas, like trees and buildings that are convenient for ninjas to climb. Thus, the world is composed of mere inspirations, mere objects, but also perversely-inspired objects, and objects which have meaningful purposes originating in some or another context of reality and psychology. Life is fundamentally both psychological and intellectual, and the true, original functionality of the world is in defiance of both ideas.

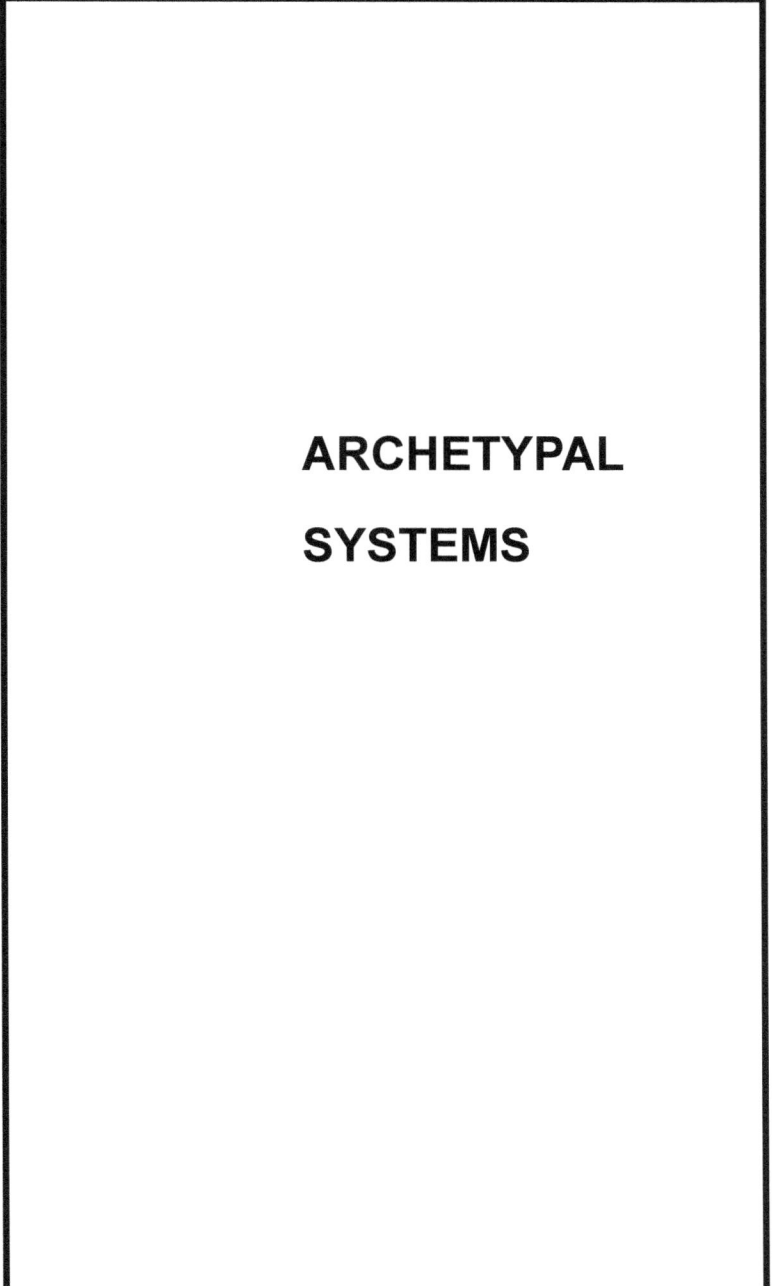

ARCHETYPAL

SYSTEMS

Nathan Coppedge

ARCHETYPAL SYSTEMS

SQUARE TEETH SYSTEMS

If you argue that something is true and something is biological as separate arguments for the idea that something is both true and biological, then this is a square-tooth argument.

Systems using square-toothed or flat arguments are distinguished from jagged tooth systems.

See Also: Jagged Tooth Systems.

ARCHETYPAL SYSTEMS

JAGGED TOOTH SYSTEMS

If you argue that something is true because it is biological, this is a causal reasoning form of jagged tooth argument.

On the other hand, if you argue that true biology is not dead, by virtue of the fact that 'not' is the opposite of 'true' and 'dead' is a possible opposite for 'biology', this is a non-causal form of jagged reasoning.

Systems using jagged tooth arguments with connected definitions are distinguished from jagged tooth arguments using essentially unrelated definitions.

However, the definition does not hold for most types of syllogisms,and not all connected arguments can be considered jagged.

Jagged implies that the argument has no extraneous parts, just connected definition words and their opposites (in non-causal reasoning), or just a series of equal defenses supporting a conclusion (causal inference).

(In my view, non-causal is more defensible and should be preferred, since it has a claim to coherency).

See Also: Categorical Deduction AND

Square Tooth Systems

ARCHETYPAL SYSTEMS

CLOSE LOGIC

Essentially the logic of collapsed systems.

For example,

One might ask 'If there is one move this system

can make, what is it?'

Or, what is the result of 'formal elapse', that is, moving from the

beginning of the implication of the system, to the end of the

implication of the system?: What is the net result from the

beginning to the end of the implication of the system?

Part of this may be:

What is the 'original' implication?

And, finally:

What is the minimum ultimate implication?

Depending on what formal tools are adopted, close logic can have

multiple type of interpretations. Most typically the formal results

are such as the following:

1. No implication. Relevance of 0.

2. Formal implication. Relevance of some type.

3. Systematic relevance. Translation or implication of some type.

4. Archetypal significance. Change of critical tools.

That's about all I can muster about close logic for now.

Basically, it deals with formal tools that are either purely

theoretical or even hypothetical. However, it has the effect of

fielding certain types of theoretical questions.

ARCHETYPAL SYSTEMS

FAR LOGIC

Far Logic, unlike close logic, is about the riskiest or most ultimate implications of a formal system.

For this reason, it tends to be more difficult to formulate.

Typically, it has two primary stages:

1. Risk, and

2. Reward.

The rationality of the risk justifies the significance of the reward. Thus, far logic tends to be rationality-intensive.

One of the primary tools often is to search for trivial results, because these results can have obvious implications without requiring excessive justification.

Systems Theory

Other methods may involve coherent logic such as categorical

deduction, paroxysm, or visual-symbolic logics like square tooth

and jagged tooth logics.

Far logics tend to be relative to the total potential of the data,

whereas close logics tend to be relative to logic ability.

As an aside, there is also a tendency in far logic to make the

system primary over the data. This has the advantage of creating

'complex alternate islands' which can be exchanged under

different localized logic paradigms (qua physics, syllogisms,

metaphysics, or coherency), so that the logic is more universal

than local physical laws.

However, in general the focus is on risk and reward, making the

system much more intuitive than simply bulk processing of
data,

or obscurantist systematizing.

ARCHETYPAL SYSTEMS

ARCHETYPAL ROOT EXPANSION

STEP 1: Identify core existing properties.

STEP 2: Decide whether the existing properties will be modified, deleted, or expanded.

STEP 3: If the properties are to be deleted, form a metaphysical theory.

STEP 4: If the properties are to be expanded, work on standardizing the archetypes for multiple levels, for example, based on a categorical or historical structure.

STEP 5: If the properties are to be modified, sketch a theory of substances and interactions.

STEP 6: Identify the root interactions, and create archetypal objects or entities that fulfill the functions of the interaction.

EXAMPLE: There is something like a water faucet. We don't know if it is highly important or not. The new object continues to exude a substance, but the substance now consists of information, rather than water. The information is real under the paradigm of combining the virtual and the physical. The creature that interacts with it knows how to bend its head, scintillate, etc. so as to interact with the information. Job done!

META THEORIES

Nathan Coppedge

Systems Theory

META THEORIES

META-CRITICISM

What makes us reject the legitimacy of a theory?

Is it that the theory must fit the relatively narrow lens of

Absolutism or the Historical?

In fact, at least one version of every theory exists, and it is the

sense of how the discipline can be interpreted or meta-critiqued.

Even things like archetypes and calculus have a meta-critique.

The more valuable a discipline, the more profound its meta theory must be.

So, let us praise applications, and consider that every discipline is really more than one sub-discipline.

And hairy will grow the fruits of knowledge!

[As prophesied in a dream]...

META THEORY

BROKEN SYSTEMS

Reference Systems: These are systems that use a broad array of

knowledge to serve one interest. They are broken in the sense

that they serve one interest or focus at a given time.

Extensional Systems: These are systems organized or developed

a certain way. They are broken in the sense that the organization

or development is not coherent, or represents a particular

vantage point.

Dominant Systems: These are systems that dominate a broad

array of information, but they remain broken and incoherent in

that the theory is often simplified and heavy-handed.

Irrational Systems: These systems make use of a highly technical interpretation to reach results about a broad array of facts. These are broken in the sense that the facts are not as technical as the interpretation, or other interpretations might exist.

Involuted Systems: These are systems in which small amounts of data are used as interpretations for larger data. These systems are broken in the sense that the smaller interpretation is not coherent, or may be unrelated to larger facts.

META THEORY

FALSE SYSTEMS

The Hanging Ropes --- People who have been to a jungle see

hanging vines. But the vines are not for swinging on. They are

just plants growing and perhaps devouring trees. People who play

at theatre also frequently see hanging ropes on a theatre set and

it becomes all-important to them. The hanging ropes in theatre

really do not express anything exceptional. They are not rational,

and confronting them always involves moving beyond them.

Motion within the ropes is literal. A little fantastic, but not

fundamentally constructive. Obsession with ropes is just

obsession. It requires work. It leads no-where outside the ropes.

The False Door --- In Egypt a false door represents the

connection to the after-life. But within other religions it

represents how Egyptians are duped. The false door is essentially

something wrong, something missing, or some form of deceit.
Like the ropes, there is no way to overcome the door except to
acknowledge what it is doing. Just as theatre is wrong for having
hanging ropes, so too Egypt is wrong for having false doors. But
unlike the ropes, a false door can mean something: it can mean
madness. And recovering from things that are missing is difficult,
but it teaches politics and sometimes philosophy.

The Cup of Joy --- Europe instead of Egypt or the theatre is
obsessed with the concept of a 'cup of joy'. Unfortunately, joy is
just indulgence, and it creates an irrational rift sort of like the
false door. Obsession with joy can take time away from
meaningful activities, and if the life and emotion fades away, then
there is nothing left. The Cup of Joy becomes the story of the
rose that was once young and fertile, but later became dried and
dead. Transient things are not really a basis for joy, but merely
foolishness. Paying for joy with misery is not a good way to
dedicate one's life. True love becomes something immortal,

instead of a fragile luxury for mortals. Learning about the real truth becomes the only way to overcome agony and hard disappointment.

The Game of Marbles --- If there is a long delay in history, it is perhaps the response to the game of marbles. This shows how the real failure is simply a lack of thought and goodness. Humanity, according to this view, remains the same as always. The scenes merely shift, but the problems remains the same. Anthropology becomes a timeless system subject to a 'logic of aberrations'. Individual taste determines the character of life, and leaves senselessness for the gods. A few prodigies survive and change from their original form. Games like marbles are timeless and influence everything while also expressing the fundamental fact that very little has changed in the mind of God. Humanity is false, so to speak. Humanity is a project. Humanity is un-thinking. Humanity is anthropology, a plastic study of games which have rules, like marbles, and stacks of marbles, and colors of marbles, etc. There is a limit to human thought because there is a limit to

the human condition. Progress involves moving beyond the human.

META THEORY

METAPHYSICS I

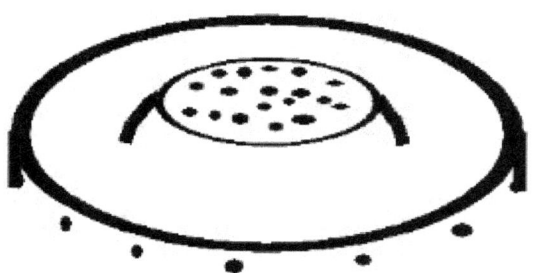

IMAGE 1: THE SEIVE THEORY

My first 'grand-unified theory' I had in college in 2001. It was based
on the idea that every type of galaxy---which I thought was a uni-
verse---was equivalent to some variation on a spindle galaxy.

Located on the ends of the central-disk structure were holes leading
to other universes. The holes were a non-objective structure, or non-
structured formula, whereas the content within the disk was structured. Also, the top and bottom of the center of the disk contained
additional holes, which particularly carried time-like strands. Thus,
the highest probability was to be located

in the intermediate area, to be transported by time in the center, or to be destroyed and re-created, on the fringe. Thus, the structure becomes a myth of creation. Overall, the theory bears some similarity to Heraclitus' theory of the sun.

IMAGE 2: HYPER-MARBLE THEORY

The second theory I also formulated in college, rarely putting it in

writing. It was a theory of objective hyper-structures called

marbles. According to the theory, the marbles were stacked

consistently, perhaps infinitely. Information sook out the marbles

for the purpose of computing. Otherwise, the purpose of the

marbles was fairly inscrutable. Although, it does bear some

145

resemblance to multi-verse theory, in this case the bubbles do not

change, but merely reflect information which serves as a variable,

resource, or element. The most serious activities take place

within the spheres, whereas much meaningless activity takes

place between them, as distinguished by the difference between

change or flux and permanence or immortality.

Qualified-Entity	Entity-qua-Entity
Qualified-Quality	Entified-Quality

IMAGE 3: RHINOS AND CAFFEINE

My first quadratic theory of exceptions was a remarkable

accomplishment. I separated all of existence into entities

('rhinos') and qualities ('caffeine'), and permuted the result.

Thus, the following categories resulted:

Systems Theory

(1) 'Doing the rhino'

(2) Rhino brand caffeine

(3) Special caffeine

(4) Caffeinated rhinos

Metaphorically, the four categories represented (I believed), an ex

clusive list inclusive of all potential categories of exceptions. Thus,

any exception, I thought, could be classified within the four things.

And, if any exception could be classified, in theory ANYTHING could

be classified that way, since, in the modern view of science, anything

is an exception, applying Meillassoux's radical contingency.

[CONTINUED...]

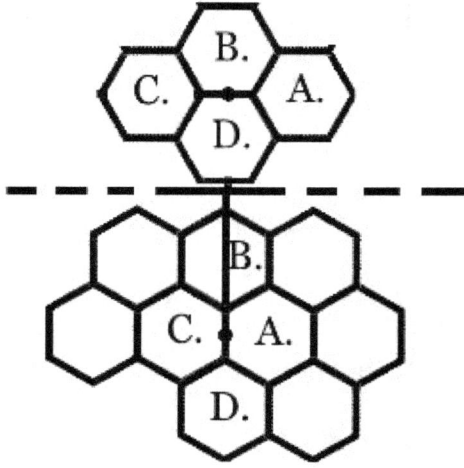

IMAGE 4: HONEYCOMB LOGIC

Perhaps realizing that there was a material debt to all this theoriz-
ing, I formulated perhaps my first genuinely material theory, which
was the theory of logically alternating honeycombs.

This was really a theory of space, rather than time or matter, and

I thought that space could do much to explain the structure of
matter. The underlying structure of space, which produces material structures based on a system of sacrifices or symmetries, goes
far in explaining the logic of material objects. For example, sex
partners are trying to resolve an underlying symmetry. Psychological problems arise out of energy imbalances, etc.

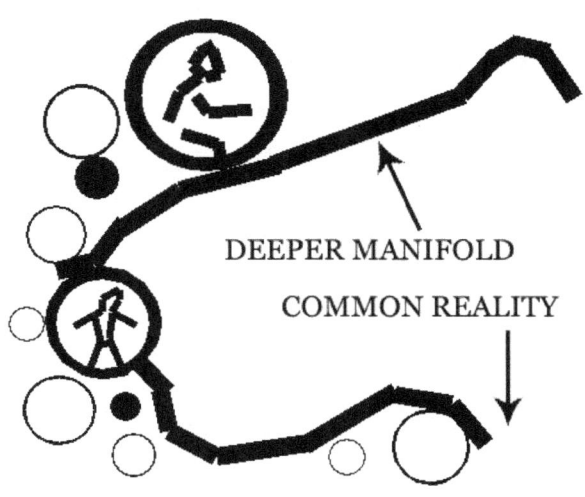

IMAGE 5: SOULS, BLANKETS, AND ORGANISMS

The 3-d reality can be used to develop souls, which are phi-losophers stones, sort of like metaphysical computers. The other elements in the fourth dimension are blankets or mani-folds, and organisms or mental / metaphysical structures.

QUALIFIED

ETHICAL

SYSTEMS

Systems Theory

ETHICAL SYSTEMS

EGALITARIANISM

Egalitarianism emerges from group-related activities, in particular transitions from one type of group to another.

Decisions are made based on the needs of the community, in terms of future and existing cultural, creative, and survival concerns.

The threat to egalitarianism comes not only through hardship and social hierarchies, but through excessive emphasis on future development, and the failure to predict the future.

One of the key properties of egalitarian studies is the tendency how each divergent axis of difficulty is counterbalanced by yet another.

Egalitarianism thus must 'secure the center': either through politics, ideas, culture, or other social strategems.

QUALIFIED ETHICAL SYSTEMS

KARMABAND

Karmaband may be stated simply as the first, original method for making bargains, sometimes known as diabolical bargains or Faustian Bargains. It is a more ethical approach than what the West today thinks along similar lines. Karmaband is an agreement in which there is a benefit in one area, and a loss in another, often opposite area.

Things considered as Karmaband may be such as the following:

*Warfare.

*Business deals.

*Intelligence (except wisdom)

*Evolution.

*Cosmetic surgery.

A karmaband is the kind of thing that comes up in certain

situations, for example: (1) When a certain result is needed, such as wishing, praying, and having physical desires, (2) When there is no certainty, for example when there is a lack of intelligence or knowledge, (3) When there is a special demand of some type, such as the need to cross a river or solve a king's problem, (4) When there is a general lack of wisdom.

Karmaband may be contrasted with practical intelligence, which is the first concept of wisdom, and the idea most frequently contrasted with evil bargains.

The folly of karmaband comes about through a misunderstanding about how one good does not guarantee another, and that only harm can happen once the good has been achieved.

Similar concepts are the Wheel of Fortune, the double-bind, and the Chinese finger-trap. The only way out is to resist!

Unlike diabolical bargains, Karmaband has a reputation for virtue.

Strategies can be produced, usually involving karma (hence the name, and through its purposive inventor, Krishna):

*Using wealth one has to benefit the poor and needy.

*Using specialized knowledge to benefit others.

*Being generous in an agreement.

*Giving ugliness a useful purpose.

*Using one's time effectively.

*Saving someone from harm.

In general, karma feels like a loss, but is actually a gain. Short-term rewards are sacrificed for long-term benefit. Meaningless things are sacrificed for significant things. Unprincipled things are

sacrificed for virtuous things. Through this principle, karma has a

reputation for sacrifice, also called karmaband.

Systems Theory

ETHICAL SYSTEMS

WISDOM

Wisdom is a much smaller system if it is broken down into exclusive categories. Understanding the general import of each category grants the fundamentals of wisdom. And since wisdom is so fundamental, on some level much of what remains is simply to indulge and ruminate on the fundamental truths, such as by asking the questions 'What?' or 'Why?'.

GENERAL WISDOM

General wisdom is knowledge of what assures and permits wisdom.

It is knowledge of the psychology and logic of wisdom. It concerns things such as human nature, age, immortality, and omniscience.

EXPERT WISDOM

Expert wisdom is the wisdom held by certain professions. It is a way to serve the interest of the self and society.

The question to ask is 'is this expertise desirable?' and 'Is it a good bargain to acquire it?'

LIFE WISDOM

Life wisdom is wisdom about the way of the world, the way of success and failure, wealth and poverty. It involves dealing with hardship, how to be comfortable, and how to overcome failure.

It often involves hard work, firm resolve, dedication to principles,

and the ability to treat oneself and others with comforts and politeness. Some spiritual leaders have concluded that ethics is the answer to life wisdom.

ADAPTATION WISDOM

Another form of wisdom is less about responding to long-term

Systems Theory

stress than it is about dealing with temporary hardship or the

unexpected. This is also called being street-smart, or evolving to cope with life's ups and downs as they happen.

As expert wisdom is to general wisdom, adaptation wisdom is to life wisdom.

ETHICAL SYSTEMS

DIRECTIONALITY

A more original idea than the categorical imperative is the idea of directed morality or directed ethics.

There are numerous approaches. One of them is the strategy of reaching things which cannot be questioned. Another is reaching things which create consistent results of some kind.

It is like a causal form of Kant's non-causal ethics. I call it merely directionality. It is a strategy that dates to Aristotle's concept of moderation, or perhaps Buddha's concept of temperance.

The realization is at least the idea that 'good habits are oft rewarded' but it is also mixed with a sense of self-sufficiency and internal mental structure.

The ethical life becomes the keystone for many other beneficial things, such as employment, happiness, or metaphysical privilege.

Continuing the ethical path becomes the means to buy into the set

of privileges without feeling desperate or naive.

In short, the ethical life becomes the good life when the person,

directed by himself or others, has directionality.

ETHICAL SYSTEMS

SELECTIVE ETHICS

The goal is to have a comprehensive body of theories to choose from.

1ST SET:

MODEL 1: Descriptor Theory

This is a basic model of language-building, inventiveness, and world-concept building. So far as I know, it underlies the current model of anthropology. It takes place through an association between the primitive concept of self, such as how you feel when you get out of bed, or how you feel when you go to a rest-stop, and actions fueled by primitive desires like thirst and vengeance. When the actions that take place through descriptor theory are formalized into people, objects, organizations, and superstitions, then we get things like science and religion, knowledge and symbolism.

Systems Theory

Critique:

MODEL 2: Functional-Purpose Theory (Teleology)

The principle of cause and effect is under-written by theories of purpose which may be more eternal. Whether the cause is natural or supernatural, the purpose or function of a thing is the simple explanation of what the thing means for us in our practical or meaningful existence. This is the primary theory that leads up to Newton's invention of the most rudimentary laws of physics.

Critique:

MODEL 3: Basic Realization Theory (Transcendentalism)

This is a theory originating with early Indian cosmologists that experience as we find it is very basic, but higher forms of existence and purpose are possible. Therefore, the life that we have as we know it is a rather basic form of existence, and the difference between our existence and the higher existence is explained by the existence of illusions. For, if higher potential is possible in the imagination, there is no reason that it would not ultimately be the case. But, since it cannot be observed in this world, it is clear that there is something (illusion) separating the many worlds.

Critique:

MODEL 4: Psychology (Ideal Materialism)

In this model, which embraces a beginning point in aesthetics, human purpose, and the rationalization of experience, the phenomena of experience (at least as we know them) are a result of actions in the mind. If there is something wrong with experience, then there is something wrong with us. Matter, if it is imperfect, is still blameless, and there is nothing to stop us from idealizing the materials we find before us. If there is something wrong with idealizing, then this does not place a limit on human happiness, but rather changes the character of the appropriate experience. The result might be something either psychic or scientific, and the duality between them is essentially a practical one.

Critique:

2ND SET:

MODEL 5: Conceptualism

Conceptualists reject the inherent descriptiveness of the world in favor of a deference to design principles. Designs may be good, or at least appear good, but that does not mean that the world itself has been perfectly designed. However, it may be that designs can contribute to a good world. And it may be practical concerns which prevent the world from appearing as if it were obviously perfectly constructed.

Critique:

MODEL 6: Cosmology

Finding an alliance between Basic Realization and

Conceptualism, Coherent Cosmologists believe that if we are not

in the right cosmos, then it is something wrong with us. In any

case, the cosmos was designed a certain way, and the differences

between one universe and another still reflect the unified vision of

God or nature. If there is something wrong with the cosmos, then

that is something interesting to study, and how we study the

cosmos and what it means reflects in the understanding of the

most meaningful purposes for humanity. What we understand

about the world influences who we are, and the limit (or

limitlessness) of our potential.

Critique:

MODEL 7: Mathematical Science

Studying the most objective properties of the world yields the

best understanding of nature, and reflects the deepest possible understanding of the intelligence found in the universe. This is the understanding of science. Mere theories, and endless unfounded variations do nothing to describe the world as it should be understood, or at least how it could be accurately represented.

Critique: The scientific view rejects the emotional view, and thus rejects a large part of the faculties of perception.

MODEL 8: Coherent Knowledge

Citing a problem with math's ability to relate with every type of thing, such as organics, human knowledge, the supernatural, and the linguistic, theories advanced by myself advocate the use of specialized knowledge applications to convey the linguistic version of the truths of nature. The application allows radical correspondence between language, nature, science, and religion concepts, by using a bounded Cartesian Coordinate System relating all properties between extremes, but excluding zero.

Critique: Critics of coherency are likely to cite its imperfection, its 'inadequacy' or non-empirical-ness, or its lack of scientific rigor.

3RD SET: (Selective ethics continued)

MODEL 9: Irrational Romanticism

Romantics say that rational claims are not the limit of known

experience. Effectively, rational concepts place a limit on what

can be known, and thus, they do not convey the 'secrets' of how

life really works. Understanding life requires moving beyond all

rational concepts, to discover the poetic, artistic, or in some other

way 'mad' concept of whatever happens to concern us. Madness

is not only a concept of the meaning of nature, but a concept of

the meaning of numbers. It has a capacity to explain anything

which is beyond reason. And it has properties that work for the

exceptional reason.

Critique: If irrationality has some legitimacy, doesn't rationality

have even more legitimacy? By the time we formalize an

Systems Theory

irrational system, haven't we got a rational system out of it?

Perhaps irrationality is only a matter of definition, whereas

rationality involves substantial concepts which can be seen

without requiring our emotions...

MODEL 10: Justice

Treating madmen like normal people has its limitations. If a large

population is mad, the result is chaos. If no justice is instilled,

civilization is corrupt, and collapses. Therefore, with or without

any concept of how nature or civilization work, there must be

some form of justice instilled to prevent utter chaos.

Critique: Elites argue that justice is not supposed to be evenly

distributed.

MODEL 11: Solipsism

Radical solipsists argue that experience is one thing, whether it is

rational or irrational, or some other thing. What defines

experience is something apart from---although chained to----our

faculty of knowledge. We should abandon the idea that these

things mean anything to those beyond us. Instead, what is

meaningful is what is meaningful for us individually.

Critique: Functionality seems to depend on accepting the reality

of other human beings. Otherwise, there is no alternative to

Utopia, which has not been seen as a functional society (it means

'No Place').

MODEL 12: Spiritualism

Rejecting every type of negativity, spiritualists find purpose in

the world's activities through the connection to the supernatural.

Critique: Some believe that the views developed by religion are

not literally true.

Systems Theory

4TH SET:

MODEL 13: Humanism

Humanism adopts a more literal view than religion, in which practical human motivations should guide all inquiries, logic, and forms of understanding. Although it seems to gamble on human development for its primary motivation, it could be argued that human development concerns everything humans are concerned with, and in this way it is a very broad concern.

Critique: Humanism may ultimately be too generic and un-creative to effect real change.

MODEL 14: Theology

The study of divinity has potential to teach what other disciplines could not teach. It seems, on the surface at least, to concern things which are of more fundamental importance than human reality.

Critique: Theologians are people who are not concerned with the practical implications of their work, but only the cloistered, spiritualized variations of arguments made by key figures who are frequently long dead. In this sense, theology does not concern a living tradition, but only tautologies.

MODEL 15: Socialism and Technocracy

Rejecting theology as impractical, socialists and technocrats focus on the practical implications of society, human problems, and sometimes, where possible, human significance. It doesn't make much difference whether humans are defined as animals, gods, humans, or post-human. What matters is how society functions, and the realizable goals and ideal conditions of social functioning. Such a system would widely accept the personal merits of people who are alive, and sometimes undergo shifts to re-envision old systems that seem out-dated. If the system works well, then the strategic shifts occur without much damage. However, this is not a Utopia, and small amounts of damage may allow the society to remain responsive to larger crises.

Critique: Some argue that a disillusioned society is not really functional, and that we may as well turn back to some form of religion.

MODEL 16: Post-Humanism

The natural development of practical humanism, post-humanism involves a society in which people become in a practical sense more-than-human. This can have a wide range of implications, but it is suspected that in some ways, barring a major crisis, post-human society will be more functional, entertaining, and intelligent than previously, in ways that are hard for previous generations to imagine.

Critique: Post-humanism is still potentially not understanding of the state of nature, and its own influence on the outcome of universal development.

5TH SET:

MODEL 17: Metaphysics (selective ethics continued)

It is argued by metaphysicians that understanding our place in

nature involves a significant degree of comprehension, and it

goes well beyond any common understanding of religion or

science. Such a view is not only practical, but also knowledgeable,

and not only knowledgeable, but functional, and not only

functional, but meaningful. Not everyone knows how to acquire

such a system, but the beginning point is a process of self-

examination.

Critique: Many argue that practical existence is always more

important, and it is usually simply sensual pleasure which leads
to

fulfillment.

MODEL 18: Hedonism

Hedonists argue that pleasure is all that is necessary for the
good

174

life. Frequently, disillusioned people will turn to entertainment as a priority, to defend them from the difficulties of life. Entertainment is an oasis, which at least appears to have a priority of serving human interest and defending the righteousness of the human.

Critique: Pleasure sometimes leads to bad consequences. Entertainment is still subject to human ugliness, stupidity, and death.

MODEL 19: Epicureanism and Aestheticism and the Immortal Quest

Epicureans reject some pleasures as un-sustainable or dangerous, and advocate the life of a secluded hermit over social indulgences. Similarly, Aesthetes favor some pleasures over others, believing the high-minded life is preferable to the 'lower life' of pigs and slobs. Raising a critique of all of the bad things in life, it is sometimes concluded that the one good thing is to pursue immortality.

Critique: It is said that Epicureans and artists are hypocrites or nihilists, and some indulgence would usually lead to more. Pleasure is the only answer to pleasure, in other words. It is argued that immortality is not achievable, and not everyone is good enough.

MODEL 20: Asceticism and Enlightenment

Abandoning pleasure---or at least pleasure as others understand it---- altogether might lead to a better life. At least, it might lead to a life without the greatest harms, like Hell or venereal disease, or God's anger. Sometimes advanced ascetics see asceticism as an alternate path to transcendence, which accepts human death, but sees another path to great spiritual accomplishment.

Critique: It is argued that asceticism is unsustainable and un-enjoyable. It looks good from the outside, but it actually is miserable. As soon as someone could enjoy the ascetic life, they could have a lot of fun doing something else. If enlightened people aren't immortal, where does that leave the rest of us? So, maybe they're doing something wrong...

6TH SET:

MODEL 21: Fascination (Child's Mind)

Some, including some scientists, and also Buddhists, have

advocated some amount of returning to child's mind, or the

fascination and imagination of the early experiences of youth.

This would serve the purpose of avoiding disillusionment,

depression, and over-thinking that might result from continually

developing adult thoughts, or becoming obsessed with advanced

ideas.

Critique:

MODEL 22: Resourcefulness / Evolution

Some have argued that flimsy answers like child's mind don't
do

enough for experience. They argue some sort of resource

adaptation is required, or some form of evolution into a new frame of mind, or a new practical ability to handle problems.

Critique: How to do this? It might not be easy, so it might be a bad idea.

MODEL 23: Genius

Rejecting many other ideas as run-of-the-mill, some see genius as the ultimate evolution currently available. In this view, the mind trumps or over-performs any other attempt to be spiritual or scientific. What can be done well by following rules can be done even better just by thinking about it. In this view, the ultimate hedonism, the ultimate religion, the ultimate science, is for the moment all about the experience and understanding of the mind / or human cognition.

Critique: Not everyone can be a genius even if they choose to be, someone might say. And if they are a genius, that doesn't mean they don't have flaws. Just because someone is a genius doesn't mean they're perfect. And, there are many people who aren't geniuses. And it's supposedly impossible to perform better than

178

anyone. So, it can't be about competition.

MODEL 24: Radical Acceptance of Passivity

Noticing the failures of many traditions, some spiritual teachers

have argued for radical acceptance of the passive condition of

life. Accepting life allows you to do anything you are capable of.
It

is also a way to psychologically adapt, and it has none of the

drawbacks of something that is a mere theory.

Critique: Many have found this adaptation hard to implement.

And some have criticized it for being morally permissive.

(END OF SELECTIVE ETHICS)

ETHICAL SYSTEMS

THE DISPUTATION

[*1] Everything right is right... This is the departure point.

[*2] Typical answers usually follow.

A. For example, there are those who will say that some things are wrong, and that the things that are right are the things that are not wrong, or not at all wrong, or at least not completely wrong...

[*3] Then there are those that will say a particular thing is right.

[*4] It will be something that appears right in itself, or at any rate which leads to some right thing inevitably, or which prevents the things which are most wrong from ever happening.

[*5] Therefore, there is a metaphysical divide, between, on the

one hand, the world in which everything wrong has been prevented, and the world in which the best things do occur. But on the other hand, there is a world where the things that are right are not particular things, but rather, merely the absence of the wrong things, and in that world, preventing the wrong things is enough to create a good world. But in the other two worlds, either there is no good object but merely much assurance about the good, or there is much good with little assurance...

[*6] Therefore, temptation is something which originally means something good, and eventually means something bad. Prevention, including moral law, is something which originally means something bad but eventually means something good. The best guess for a good life (at first) is merely to avoid problems, which leads to enough knowledge to predict that the good comes later. In that way, temptation is sacrificed for the sake of knowledge. Likewise, psychic knowledge---knowledge that arrives early---must be very good. For it is like good things which have arrived early, because at first there was not enough knowledge to declare that it was good.

181

[*7] Knowledge, then is the simple form of the good life.

[*8] Therefore, developing knowledge can lead to a better life,
since developing what is good causes it to be more good than
before. Then, in one sense, what is morally good is what is
good
as a development of knowledge. It might be, for example, that it
is good to live a good life, meaning a life that has knowledge.
Such a life has an implication of a correlation between ethical
conduct and knowledge, which might be called meaning.

[*9] But, what does this knowledge-development consist of? It
may easily consist ---- at least in some sense --- of the corollary
for ethical conduct, that is, meaning. But it is not meaningful
automatically in every case.

[*10] What is meaningful automatically is the ethical world: the
world that is both a paradise, and in which no harm could occur,
not even a perversity, not even an undesirable thought.

182

Systems Theory

[*11] What is less automatic is the meaning in an unethical world. And I find that in this world, there is greater perversity, and since some things are not desirable, the perversity naturally (the majority of the time) concerns perverting the bad things that might occur, so that they do not occur. Therefore, rules such as leisure, thought-for-its-own-sake, and the appreciation of irony and paradox occur. Further, where this world becomes the model for some better world, it is because these models of behavior have been preserved in some form. Whereof, symbolism might arise to guarantee the good things from out of what once was bad, like a lion that is no longer ferocious, perhaps because the good times have come again.

[*12] However, there is no certainty that these ironic virtues are not virtuous. Particularly, they ARE virtuous relative to the world in which they are found.

A. It is false to premise that ignorance is the condition of a world in which cruelty dominates, as cruelty will make the sour conditions of the world all the more clear. Perhaps the best and goodest things are not present, and so the person is ignorant of those things. But those things may have been merely writings, thoughts of a better world, which occurred during a time of ignorance in which even cruelty was not clear enough. Or perhaps the writer was someone who experienced much pleasure and became ignorant of cruelty, or who became deranged from a noble desire to overcome the 'petty' problems of the world through politics, or some other high-minded activity. We cannot excuse the past by thinking that it was a time of better things. But we can excuse the present for its having to confront what now seems cruel. But, we should not compromise the virtues that remain in the world...

[*13] The virtue of the world which is not automatically virtuous is the non-automatic virtue, which is philosophy.

[*14] However, exceptional virtues exist in exceptional worlds. But these exceptions imply worlds of their type.

Systems Theory

A. Either the worlds are being created anew, or they implicate some pre-existing trend which might be judged as to whether it is good. Specifically, if these virtues are so exceptional, why are they not difficult, or why are they so-actually good, when some other virtues are easier? Why do they offer the most good thing? Or is it only because they are exceptional? If they are 'only exceptional' then why is it not merely the exceptional world that is good? But is the exceptional world metaphysically good? Or is the virtue of the exceptional world a material virtue? Or is it some exception with materialism? Apparently, the exceptional world concerns the special properties of materialism (such as music), a value that reduces to objects, a metaphysical virtue, or mere exceptionism. Otherwise, what is offered is a difficult or exceptional virtue. So, in any case, the exceptional world must express rare or exceptional virtues, judging by the idea that objects themselves are rarifications. Otherwise, what is expressed by exceptions is simply common objects.

[*15] There must be some way that philosophy occurs which makes it good. But if it is not an exceptional good, then it must be

a common good.

[*16] The ethos of philosophy therefore concerns some common good, or else some exceptional good.

[*17] Where philosophy is granted a metaphysical exception for being non-automatic virtue, then philosophy may already constitute an exceptional ethos, without granting exceptionism to the subjects it concerns.

[*18] Philosophy may also concern a common domain of exceptions where specific conditions of reality are applied. Thus, philosophy may concern the rules of reality, whether they are physical, metaphysical, or purely exceptional.

[*19] Thus, so far as real exceptions tend towards the universal, the common good may be concerned with physical, metaphysical, and exceptional rules of reality, or else the general ethos of philosophy.

[*20] Where physics does not constitute rules, the rules are likely to be exceptions to physics.

[*21] Where philosophy does not constitute rules, the broken rules are likely to be physical exceptions.

[*22] Therefore, philosophy may aspire to be physical or else introduce an exceptional metaphysics.

A. Philosophers such as Iris Murdoch and Immanuel Kant have been fond of the term 'Metaphysics of Morals' to explain how metaphysics is a figure of morals, morals being a greater expression of the vagueries of a metaphysical principle. In this sense, ethics is an explanation.

[*23] The opportunity is then for some sub-domain of philosophy to constitute morals, such as logic, politics, or consciousness.

[*24] Therefore, tentatively, immorality concerns three things.

A. Irrationality.

B. Political Crimes.

C. Unconsciousness.

[*25] If that is the case, the middle world concerns the three positives already introduced.

A. Logic.

B. Politics.

C. Consciousness.

[*26] Virtues in the land of fulfillment therefore concern the following.

A. Pleasures proven by logic.

1. Fulfillment.

2. Ideas.

3. Justice.

4. Meaning.

B. Political virtues.

Systems Theory

1. Democracy.

2. Meritocracy.

C. Higher consciousness.

[*27] Additionally, philosophy might be an important virtue.

(END OF THE DISPUTATION)

ETHICAL SYSTEMS

HYPOCRISY

HYPOCRITICAL KNOWLEDGE

There comes a time in a conversation with a priest, a therapist, or some other expert, when you can no longer believe what they tell you.

It is approximately the point at which they continue to spout their usual, but a time at which you yourself have already been practicing remarkable achievements. It is the time of achieving prodigal greatness, but it is also the time when one should realize the world's disappointment.

I came to this conclusion in talking to a therapist who was in graduate school for Divine Knowledge. He was, all in all, a very ethical person. He appeared to have a restrained marriage with a white woman. His story was one of success. He once won a $100,000 grant to do social work.

Systems Theory

What I noticed was this: he had been overcome by the incidious evil of his work place: the fact that a large number of the clients smoked cigarettes. In spite of his professed allergy to cigarettes, he had become addicted to second-hand smoke. Although I saw the symptoms also in myself, I wondered why this therapist thought his work was so important if in this one way he had compromised his health.

It is a typical case of hypocrisy. He was spouting on about virtuous behaviors because of an incidious un-resolved problem that caused him to exaggerate the importance of what he was saying. He had become vain, because he thought his work was great. But he thought his work was great because he was addicted to secod-hand smoke.

There are at least four types of hypocrisy that I have discovered:

1. The hypocrisy of desire. Desiring effects rather than truths.
2. The hypocrisy of dishonesty. Fooling oneself or others.

191

3. Hypocrisy of insidious evil. Denying truth's importance.

4. The hypocrisy of professionalism. Acting.

Systems Theory

ETHICAL SYSTEMS THEORY

METAPHYSICS II

First called this name by Aristotle in the West, metaphysics is not always considered a system, and bears some resemblance not only to Eastern views of a similar kind, perhaps generally known as 'cosmology' or 'cosmogyny' or 'the knowledge of things', but also to the mathematical concept of the lemma, through the relation of material science to spiritual and abstract matters purportedly beyond ordinary conception.

The overall concept of metaphysics tends to be additive rather than singular. Concepts like knowledge, physics, God, and technology have had huge influences at various times, often continuously. There is a danger of losing large concepts like these in 'mere inflections' which amount to the preference of one power of explanation over another. The absurd greatness of existence is one matter, and arriving at a rational explanation is another. Technology might not mean as much as we think it does,

193

but it certainly means more than what we use to think, unless
existence as we know it is an illusion.

Illusion has been one of the earliest dominant concepts in
metaphysics, and it is associated with the most profound power of
creating everything that appears for mortals. Another concept
that has major importance is the containment of the large within
the small, the sense of how ordinary values are compromised
when they come up against something larger, more powerful, or
more magical. Simultaneously, norms of technology have done
much to replace the assumption of a magical foundation with
something more like economics, suggesting that the more magical
realities are locked off from ordinary mortal existence,or only
exist through hallucination.

Finally, we can consider that there are at least four or more major
approaches to metaphysics, regardless of the specific perception
of reality:
1. Monumental Metaphysics (the metaphysics of Creation): In
this view, the ontology is a growth process as of larger and

smaller men, and everything that is most true is constructed painstakingly from infinite smaller parts---which together constitute the essences of life. Pain in this view is an explanation for differences in greatness, necessary actions, and so on and so on. The major scheme is teleology, but it is progressive. It simply exists in a very large time scale, and many progressions and digressions can occur for any one person. The highest good is wisdom. This view might be critiqued as idealistic. Every good seems to come from someplace better, indefinitely. This is the view favored by philosophers, prophets, and architects. The good is the great project.

2. Mystery Metaphysics (the metaphysics of Kings): This is a pluralist view that holds that many different 'gods' and 'treasures' deserve venerable worship. Life is the explanation of the relation between the 'people' and 'treasures' of importance and the common people, who seek to attain possession of those objects and attributes. In this view, pain is explained as the struggle for (often temporary) worth and purpose. Practicality and admirableness are high virtues, but ultimately so is magic. This

view might be critiqued as materialistic or obscure. Life seems to

exist as a kind of exception, a mysterious chance happenstance.

This is the view favored by psychics, alchemists, and buddhists.

Evil is a type of expense.

3. Animated Metaphysics (the metaphysics of Middle Earth):

This is one of the possible divine views of metaphysics. The world

responds to one's special desires, made possible by the Mandate

of Heaven or Divine Contract. Through the lens of this privilege,

the world 'talks back' and magic can be evoked and created. This

is the view of Egyptian Pharaohs, Chaldean sorcerers, yogis, and

some Greek magic practitioners. The greatest good is attained by

those with the greatest rights, and lost for those without rights.

Evil is something that happens when there is a lack of skill or

lack of divine Justice.

4. Illusionary Metaphysics (Practical metaphysics): This is simply

the collection of realities that exist by the relation of experience

to the unreachable experiences, often described by Karma.

Essentially, there are laws that determine what feelings and aspects of the world are available at a given time. One can guess from others' great achievements that they have different, more desirable realities. It is the work of virtue to aspire to attain the same greatness in the world, or in the spiritual world. Commonly this view is mistaken for simply the spiritual side of life. But, it actually determines material attainments just as well. One must assume that kings have different options than the common man. But the difference is that the king must obey a contract. The common man is free, although the common man is less fortunate. Pain in this view is contact with baseness, and evil is association with base people.

Since these seem like ethical perspectives more than logical ones, I will post metaphysics as an ethical system rather than a formalistic one.

QUALIFIED ETHICAL SYSTEMS

DOXOLOGIC

Doxologic or Logical Doxology comes from the Greek meaning

Doxo- meaning a cultured body of beliefs or opinions.

Doxology thus relates with the concept of consumed knowledge, specifically knowledge derived from experiences such as traditions, gossip, and degrees of localized knowledge.

In my own variation of logical doxology, called objectivistic doxology or just Doxologic, the objectivity of sources of belief are brought into question, and a groundwork is attempted to be established unifying certain classifications of words and experiences through the use of categories.

The most basic technique is to find a statement that appears to provide a basis of knowledge, and then to simply determine what things about the statement determine that it is objective.

Instead of questioning the specific premises as to whether they are true, an objective Doxologist will almost always adopt relative absoluteness, meaning that the statement must be true in some way. This can be taken as a first principle.

Systems Theory

A related principle is the idea of majority absurdity, which is that the majority of statements must be considered ridiculous, and thus, since statements serve as the objective grounding of another statement, even the sources of truth related to a given statement are mostly ridiculous.

This may be compared to the experience of Robinson Crusoe on a desert island. Normally when we hear that a president is elected, we say 'That is wonderful, because I'm a Democrat'. Or, 'That is wonderful, because I'm a Republican'. But Robinson Crusoe must say that 'That is ridiculous'. Not because electing presidents is ridiculous to everyone, but because the election is ridiculous to him personally, because he is stuck on a desert island.

The objective doxologist argues that the same is true for anyone about anything, in some degree. Since most statements about a given thing are ridiculous, those people who experience the true meaning of words are themselves on a desert island in which all foreign information contradicts them. The difference is that the true meaning of words finds rationality within the absurdity.

Thus, there are a number of primary positions on doxologic:

1. Perhaps life is completely absurd, because there is no inherent rationality to anything. This is the position taken by Camus in his novel The Stranger.

2. Perhaps meaning is arbitrarily constructed, and there are multiple ways of interpreting what is best or even what is most enjoyable. This is the position taken by Sartre and the Post-Modernists.

3. Perhaps one thing is more true than another, although each thing is the best example of itself. This is the position taken by the Platonists.

4. Perhaps all things are true in some way, and no truth can be preferred over another because they are all equally true. This is

the position taken by relativists.

Ironically, in some ways relativism is the most objective view in this sort of Ontography. By the time one thing is true, then it requires an ethical purpose, which suggests that meaning is individual and thus arbitrarily constructed (because multiple people can be right, but about different things that demand the same resources), and that returns us to the idea that all things are absurd, and that, ironically, everything is equally true.

The position of the objective doxologist is really an objective interpretation of the interconnection between these four areas. Thus, it may involve the following:

1. Proof of the desirability of absurdity or some specific emotion which is not exactly absurd --- since absurdity is too absurdly narrow to mean anything.

2. Finding an un-evaluated meaning or affirmation within a given experience, possibly leading to naive realism or emotivism.

3. Open-ended evaluation of objects as they correspond to their environment, what has been called remedial studies, for example in architecture or cultural theoretics. This involves the evaluation of what norms and deviations mean in spite of changes in society.

4. Perhaps a rule can be defined that applies to all aspects of a given object or society. In this case, there could be an ethical paradigm that could be used as a rule of thumb until there is a paradigm shift.

So, further concepts include:

Paradigm Shift: A categorical change to all of society.

Remedial Studies: Re-evaluation of the relevance of trends.

Naive Realism: Belief that things are physically as they appear.

Narrowness: Limitation of any given term in overall description.

That concludes this somewhat intermediate approach to doxology.

Beyond this level, things tend to get pretty deep, or the questions remain unresolved!

Systems Theory

QUALIFIED ETHICAL SYSTEMS

PLANAR TRANSCENDENCE

Some ethical systems involve the interaction between multiple levels or degrees of reality. More conventionally, they would be called metaphysical systems. But that application is very rough.

Planar transcendence is more like an existential tool than a metaphysical system.

Some examples present themselves:

1.   The control of demons by the Star of David.

2.   The achievement of Nirvana by Buddhas.

3. God's division between the heavens and the earth.

4. The stories of creating perfect works of art.

5. The story from 1001 Arabian Nights of the 7 Seals of Solomon.

6. The story of animating a clay golem.

What is common to all of these stories is a kind of personal mindful mastery, which then applies to the world over which one has argued to become ruler.

For example,

Harmless knowledge = ruler of hell.

Worldly knowledge = realm of Nirvana.

Completeness of soul = dividing heaven and earth.

Idiosyncracy = creating perfect works of art.

Magic of the immediate = traveling to see the ultimate.

Total spiritual knowledge = giving life to clay.

These explanations are but bits and pieces of something which remains inaccessible in the third dimension.

A frequent motif of these things is additional powers like flight and invisibility. Perhaps they would be common fare in the fourth or fifth dimension. For reasons like this, unlocking further dimensions has been an argument for their possibility. Yet, questioning the universalism of the next world by opening a portal

might have the effect of canceling the power. By this argument it must be seen that ignoring the laws of the realm is either fool-hardy, or brings punishment.

Another factor may be that there are systems of attainment to reach high levels of various occult disciplines. Some of these levels are described in The Yoga Sutras of Patanjali, and in the Alchemical Levels.

Systems Theory

IMPARALLEL REALIZATION

Imparallel realization is the type of insight, not exclusively

ethical, but often ethically loaded, in which decisions in one place are different in some way from decisions in another place.

Typically this is explained in terms of the ethical division of the world, but if the world is not seen as ethically divided, then it can take place through other paradigms, such as survival (pragmatism), manners (act low amongst the low) and architectural 'program' (design according to the surrounding setting).

Opposite realizations are also part of imparallel realization, such as deadly obstacles (what happens if your helmet shatters in outer space), immature manners (the obligation to act polite), and objective design (design according to materials). The perversion of the ethical version of imparallel realization would be some kind of diabolical reasoning, like 'hell belongs in heaven' instead of 'the devil belongs in hell'. The ethical insight would be that one should be the best thing in the worst circumstances, instead of being punished according to one's desserts.

The amazing thing is all of this might be ONE ethical system: the system of applied ethics and location, which can not only accept ethical principles, but also see the twisted variations of them.

ETHICAL SYSTEMS

INTELLECTUAL MORALS

Intellect is in one sense, a path of striving.

But, it is only genuine when it has already been achieved.

The importance, then is in forming a rational system.

But as soon as we can be responsible for such a system, we can also be responsible for destroying it.

All amounting to: thoughts are big. We can be blamed for our thoughts. Thinking of good things might be selfish. Thinking of bad things might be foolish.

ETHICAL SYSTEMS

EXCEPTIONAL MORALITY

What you would do to no one never happens to you at that time!

Where you grant yourself exceptions, you lose account of the good.

What is perfect is at least not at all negative.

Truth aspires to the good.

Truth is ideally permanent.

ETHICAL SYSTEMS

GUILT BY ASSOCIATION: PRIESTHOOD 1

Someone makes a dirty offering, and they are first to call it an offering, and they are first to call it 'dirty'.

They are also first to deny that it is an offering to the gods.

But this 'priest' is like a priest, and yet a real priest is associated by moral concern: he only becomes guilty by judging and helping people.

In every case, it is the person concerned who is concerned.

There is something to be said simply for the guilt of association.

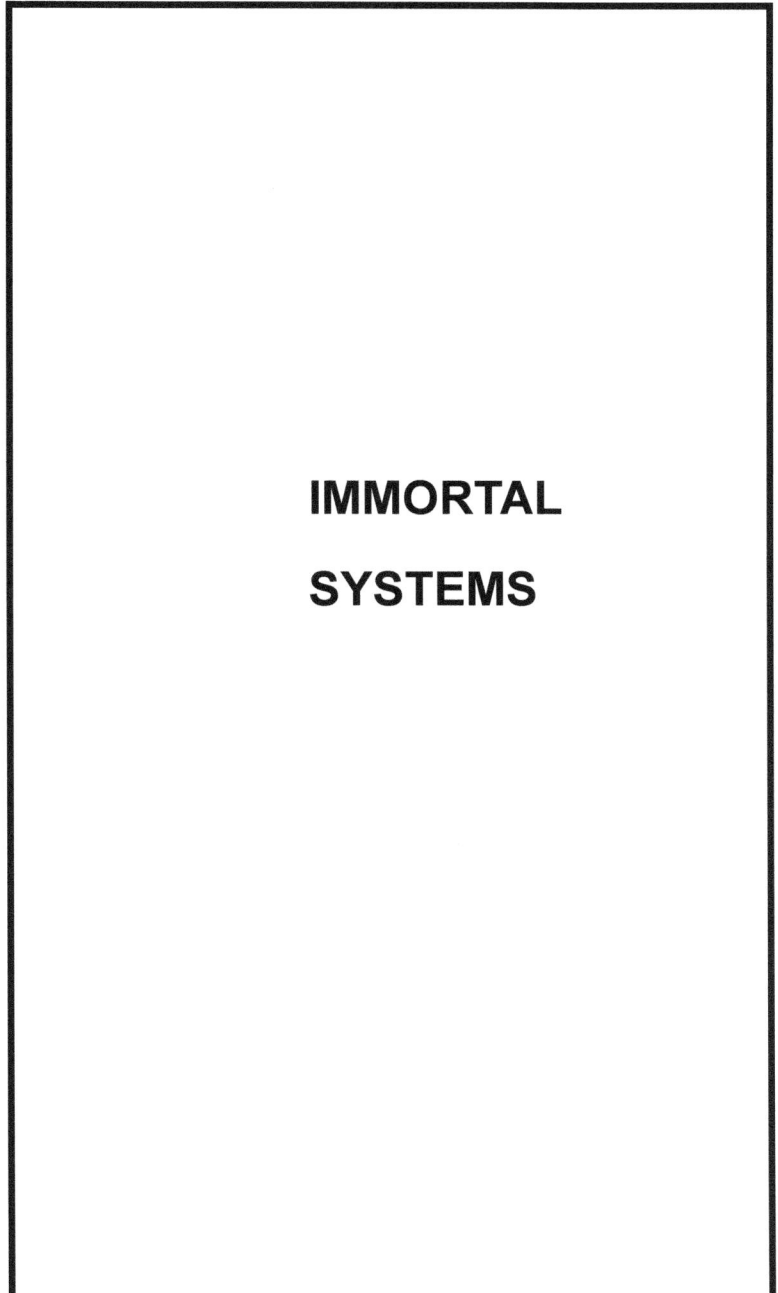

IMMORTAL

SYSTEMS

Nathan Coppedge

Systems Theory

IMMORTAL SYSTEMS

USINEOSIS

Usineosis means "No age / agelessness". Here is a short

writing abbreviating my first major clues about its

coherent meaning:

A. The easy is not hard: Relax as much as possible.

B. Hard is easy: Have a principle of longevity.

C. What is not easy is not hard: Make adaptive selections.

D. Easy is hard: Live long.

This might be a major clue about the system called anti-aging.

It is a response to a bus driver talking about someone who had

Alzheimer's, and how it wasn't a good way to die. Translating the

above, one should relax and feel stupid sometimes so as not to

over-stress the brain. This can reduce risk of 'brain-pressure' that can lead to Alzheimer's. The principle of longevity keeps the

brain in a patient, long-endurance state that is more adapted to

having high-functionality experiences late in life: 'continue

thinking about the future!' Making adaptive selections is an

extension of the principle that leads to eating healthy foods and

avoiding discomfort and other negative conditions that could

make one become more mentally passive. The ultimate lesson is

'live long', and this can be relative within trying circumstances,

but becomes more objective if someone reaches 80 - 120.

Take these lessons seriously!

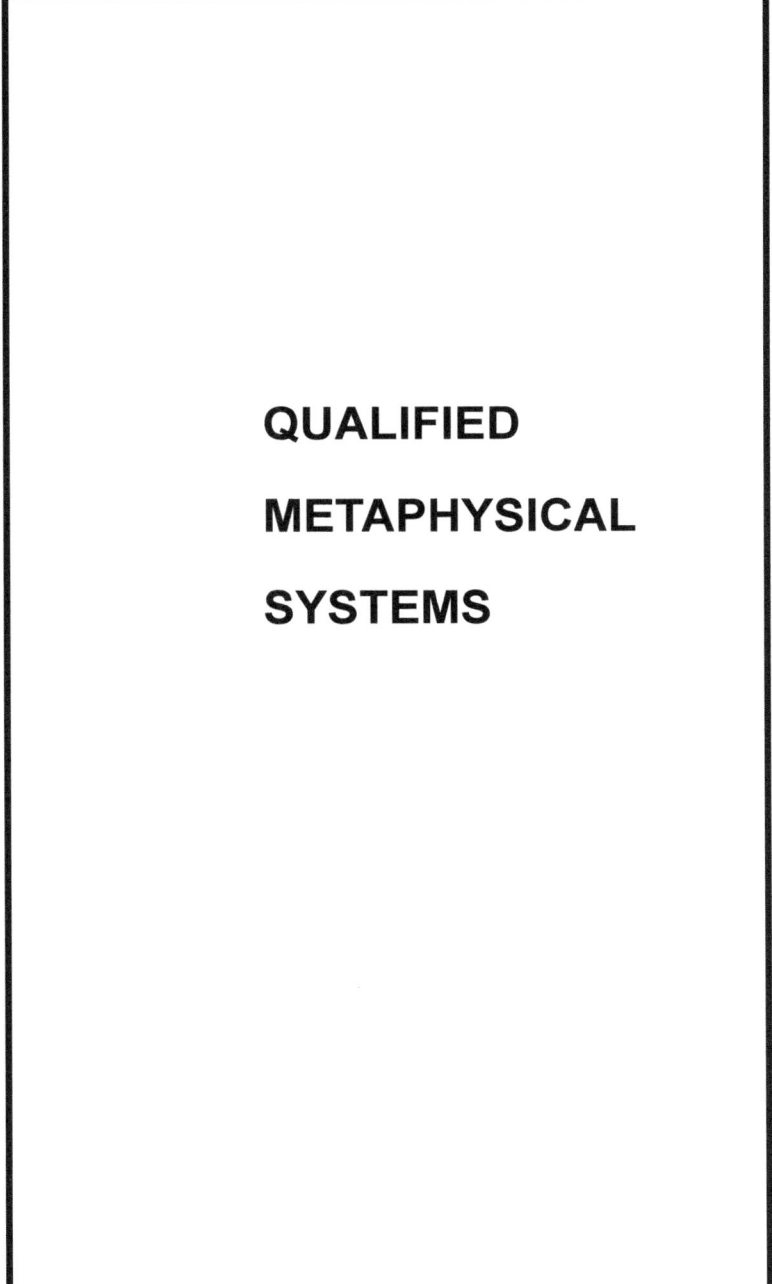

QUALIFIED

METAPHYSICAL

SYSTEMS

Nathan Coppedge

Systems Theory

METAPHYSICAL SYSTEMS

ERSATZ METAPHYSICS

Someone may ask someone else: "What is your first theory?" And when there is an immediate answer, that means that they have already considered the complex, the ersatz.

When the answer is a form of metaphysics, then they have considered ersatz metaphysics.

Oftentimes the answers are NOT a complete metaphysics.

There are many other theories that go un-named. And when we don't know what they are, then we are having a thought about ersatz metaphysics.

It is not something easy to know, but when we have knowledge of Socratic ignorance (if such is possible) we can hypothicate other worlds in a purely hypothetical manner, and this is how we are led to ersatz metaphysics.

Ersatz metaphysics has at least the following properties:

1. Consideration of the absurd.

2. More than one hypothesis.

3. Doubt about which theory is correct.

4. Sheer imagination.

Maybe that is all apart from the theories and their propensive validity.

METAPHYSICAL SYSTEMS

THE NORMA

Euclid defined a symbol today known as a grid of equal-sized squares. It was called a 'norma'.

The norma figures in metaphysics as an early training lesson.

It has a few typical successive stages, but exceptions may be made in exceptional circumstances:

1. Exploration of the norma: such as an ant. The norma is interpreted in some way, sometimes with difficulty.

2. Artistic endeavors. The person tries to do better than the norma, and often can't. However, eventually they succeed in making quality art and pass this level.

Systems Theory

3. Encounter with the norma: the figure re-emerges, often as a

symbol of some type, rationalized by the individual. The earlier

this confrontation happens and the more successful the outcome,

the sooner the person passes basic metaphysics.

Some categories to consider:

A. The metaphysical dunce. Someone who adopts the norma
as a

religious symbol unthinkingly.

B. The eschatologist. Someone that studies the religious

significance of the symbol, but does not see its metaphysical

importance.

C. The philosopher, logician, or metaphysician. Someone that

sees the symbol has metaphysical significance, but cannot always explain why.

D. The wizard or sage. Someone that has moved beyond The

Norma.

METAPHYSICAL SYSTEMS

PHILOSOPHICAL REALISM

This may involve:

*Classical variablism (proto-dimensionalism or simulacra).

*4-d paradises.

Systems Theory

METAPHYSICAL SYSTEMS

WIZARD METAPHYSICS

This is guesswork based on some of my most advanced studies.

Part I. General Overview

Wizard metaphysics begins when everything is made of intelligence, to such a degree that reality is not the proper name for everything.

You see, reality comes in degrees. And it is the profit of the wizard to know what to do with reality.

The wizard learns the ethics of modality, or he learns to break the rules. If the wizard grants himself enough exception in such a world, he may have his own residence and grow rich.

Otherwise, without exception, he may become enslaved to laws, either of this realm or some other.

Exceptions are a matter of intelligence, but so, too, are laws. The life of the wizard is both 'free' and 'reasoned'. He discovers 'matters' (querrels, problems) on the realm of reason.

If he encounters trouble, he may choose to conceal his form, change shape, re-locate, or become disenchanted and fallen within his creations.

Part II. As-A-Wizard

Progress occurs not only within alchemical levels (which are in their spiritual sense rather juvenile), but also within life-arc progressions which may be recognized through sudden epiphanization.

Before real wizardry is realized, significant skill developments may be enclosed like a nested egg within larger dramatic arcs setting off confrontations with external powers.

For example, if someone has real aptitude, the confrontation becomes one with magical thieves or 'borrowers' who must be connived and bargained with before the skills are realized again. This was my experience.

My first encounter with wizardry was as a kind of superficial

Chinese god who had several powers, including a one-time masterful invisibility, flying jump, and raise dead (self). However, it was not for another nine reincarnations before I even recognized wizard power again. And, when I did, it was much weakened.

The beginning of my arc could be described as 'the beginning of myself' and the end could be described as 'the end of myself'. However, what I mean by this is nothing more than a particular arc of my magical education. In the beginning, in my fourth life, I had ridiculous powers but little ability to critically examine them. Now, in my 13th life I have the ability to imagine what a wizard world would be like. My powers are weakened, and I have adopted philosophy as a crutch.

The word 'Engymion' describes the next major stage in my magical education, a stage that will only occur if I once again succeed in attaining prolonged life.

METAPHYSICAL SYSTEMS

STATUES MODEL

Statues appear to explain the current model of metaphysics, in which the Earth revolves around the Sun, and figures walk on the Earth.

The figures walking are clearly the fantasy of statues, little more intelligent than this.

The Earth is clearly the statue's thought of a larger statue, whichis doing all that a statue can imagine it would do: to support the smaller statues.

The Sun may be explained as the eye looking upon the statues.

So, the entire local scene is explained in terms of statues! If we are statues, then it can be argued that there is no coincidence that we feel pain in our brain! After all, what we think of as our brain is really solid rock!

Elidian Leap: Perhaps, however, this is really just one version of metaphysics for 3-d. Elements such as organs (eyes, etc.), centers, orbits, and affinities may explain some variations of metaphysics.

METAPHYSICAL SYSTEMS

NON-IDENTITY THEORY

If every identity is in some way self-fulfilling, and self-identifying, that is, if it serves as its own fulfillment network, and the limit of fulfillment is the limit of self-identity, then:

It may be that if we look at everything that does not concern our own identity, we see things that are never fulfilled.

And these things, since they are never fulfilled, are never identities.

At least, they are not identities to us, when we are lost, nor are they identities to us when we are fulfilled, as some gods have discovered.

METAPHYSICAL SYSTEMS

STRING THEORY

When I learned the basics of calculus, I also learned how to have insights into string theory.

My first idea was the equal-energy particle theory = string theory, which at least sounds similar to other string theories. From the theory of equal energy, we can get concepts such as supersymmetry, singularity, and virtual singularity (informational vectors), which suggests that the theory actually is a form of string theory, although perhaps a misguided one.

METAPHYSICAL SYSTEMS

PLENUM-NOT-PLANET THEORY

"It is not a planet, but a plenum". The theory that planets are gods was respected by the ancient Greeks, but the theory was not widely entertained recently, since planets were not literally gods.

But, the theory of volitional mechanics lent some credence to the theory. According to volitional mechanics, energy, force, energy force, or momentum can come from nothing other than mass.

Therefore, there is some reason to believe that planets move of their own volition, albeit because of interactions between lower-dimensional and higher-dimensional properties.

The theory would also explain the difficulty in rationalizing human actions in terms of just chemistry or food consumption.

APPLIED

SYSTEMS

Nathan Coppedge

Systems Theory

APPLIED SYSTEMS

ADVANCED CONCEPT ANALYSIS

STEP 1: Briefing.

A dense packet of information is provided, from one paragraph to many pages.

For example,'

'Substance X is under investigation for its potential advantages as a life-extension supplement. Although it is proven to extend life in rats, the substantiation of the claim is in question. Specifically, the drug appears to have many of the side effects of a drug called amphetamine. Sorting out whether the drug is viable depends on determining that the drug has no major dependency and does not pose a risk to the vital organs.'

STEP 2: Risk Assessment.

Does the project in question pose a risk personally, psychologically, financially, nationally, or globally? Then the project must be considered carefully, and possibly rejected.

In our example, the answer would be something like:

Be serious, after all, if it has the same side effects it is likely to be the same drug. We may already have to control for existing dependencies.

STEP 3: Available Alternatives

Is the project indispensable in some way?For example, is it serving some larger agenda?For example, some students may feel amphetamines are worth taking for short-term performance boosts.

STEP 4: Spin.

What is the best interpretation of all the facts?

Can the project be interpreted positively or negatively?Does the spin have a function?

For example, advertising boosted performance may boost perform-ance even if no one takes the drug ('grass is greener effect').

STEP 5: Responsible Actions.

What can be done to advance the agenda of the concerned individu-als, businesses, the nation, or the world?

Should there be a cleanup program, a business agenda, a production line, or government oversight?

Resolving these questions determines the ultimate importance of the project, not immediately, and not automatically, but gradually.

For example, maybe amphetamines should be regulated, but permit-ted as performance boosters for those that want them and are aware of the risks. Meanwhile, the search continues for an immortality drug.

Systems Theory

APPLIED SYSTEMS

ORIGINAL GEOGRAPHY

1. The elongated world of perception --- extension into distances.

2. The perceptions watching over the world --- perhaps birds or

God.

3. The mechanical world lying just underneath --- the mind, the

city, the animals. The populations of nature. The islands that can

be navigated.

4. The dead world: the world of the battlefield, amorphous,

smoke-stranded. Also the immortal world in which other beings

pass away.

APPLIED SYSTEMS

MACROSCOPY

In the philosophical sense that I understand it and interpret it,
macroscopy or macro-vision is the ability to find greater
relevance within the existing experience or existing environment.

It has several kinds.

Specifically:

Scientific macroscopy: literally seeing the larger world, as
through a large telescope. This may be the level in which the
universe is understood literally or mathematically. The general
study scientifically can be called 'macroscience'.

Creative macroscopy: interpreting objective arts that would
otherwise remain unknown. This is the level of creativity in which

the created object is of a style of such importance that the style is objective. It may be literature, visual art, the shape of a sculpture, a large body of music taken together, etc. The general form of creative knowledge can be called macro-creativity.

Spiritual macroscopy: revelations about God or the plan of the universe. These are typically things deemed to have timely relevance to humanity. The general domain of spirituality can be called macro-spirituality.

Existential macroscopy: revelations about one's own life or sense of self-purpose or relevance to the universe. This may take the form of having a mission in life, a calling to a specific kind of work, or a unique ability. It can be called discovery of macro-existence.

APPLIED SYSTEMS

BASIC PROPERTY ANALYSIS

Malleability --- can the object be twisted or torn?

Structural soundness --- is the object well-built?

Basic function --- is the object designed for a game, writing,

assembling, visualizing, as a piece of clothing, etc.?

Advanced function --- does the object serve as a computing or

calculating device, as a clock or timepiece, etc. Does it have

hidden functions which are part of it's overall designed purpose?

Un-obvious basic function --- does the object serve as

camouflage, for confusion, distraction, or transformation of itself

or some other object?

Un-obvious advanced function --- can the object be interpreted
to

have importance (logically, scientifically, etc.) for the utter

advance of civilization?

Systems Theory

APPLIED SYSTEMS

IDEA MECHANICS

Let's consider hypothetically that someone doesn't believe

Atheism is a difficult idea. For a long time they consider atheism

in a thoughtless way: a part of their life.

But at some point, someone introduces the idea that atheism

could be a difficult concept. Maybe a concept that requires a

divinity.

At this point a strategy is needed. Perhaps, instead, atheism is a

result of human inventiveness. But is human inventiveness easy

or difficult? Wouldn't difficult inventiveness be inspired? And

wouldn't easy inventiveness involve an overflow of many

concepts, no individual one of them of which could be preferred?

Apparently, the atheist has a choice: either atheism has divine importance (a singular concept), or humanity was divinely

inspired to think of it!

This is the kind of argument that underlies idea mechanics, a discipline that has existed in some form for a long time, perhaps since the invention of ideas concept in language in Ancient India or Athens.

The point is, until we recognize that an idea IS an idea, in a divine

sense, then we don't have much power over it.

So, there are four basic categories of idea mechanics:

1. Inspired ideas (divine origin).

2. Logic (favoring one theory over another).

3. Semantics (multiplicity of theories), and:

4. Objectivity (perfect knowledge).

Systems Theory

APPLIED SYSTEMS

NEWTON'S LAWS OF MOTION

An object in motion tends to stay in motion.

Every action has an equal and opposite reaction.

Motion continues unless there is resistance.

These laws continued to be seen as having universal relevance until Quantum Mechanics came along, and determined the laws to be different at different scales. Nonetheless, Newton's Laws of Motion tend to remain accurate at what we call intermediate scales, or some say, above the atomic level.

APPLIED SYSTEMS

THE LAWS OF THERMODYNAMICS

0: That, all conditions being equal, energy remains constant.

1: That, with some resistance, energy decreases.

2: That, with heat energy, energy tends to dissipate.

3: That, since most structures have some void, no perfect seal

can be built to contain heat.

4: That, over infinite time, energy tends to return to zero.

5: That energy tends to be created from the destruction of

particles.

These may not be the official definitions, but they give an clear

overview of the types of concepts covered by Thermodynamics.

Systems Theory

APPLIED SYSTEMS

WEAPON SYSTEMS

Weapon systems have broad application to role-playing and national defense. Many defense technologies have later been adapted to civilian and aeronautics roles, including mass manufacturing, plastic, lightweight metals, airplanes, and nuclear technologies.

Here are two examples of military technologies, specifically weapon systems, that may be capable of inspiring another technology, perpetual motion machines:

(1) The OICW, or Objective Infantry Combat Weapon is a weapon developed relatively recently compared to other rifles and grenade launchers. It may be based on a drawing I made in middle school or high school using a similar design:

The concept was to combine a pump grenade launcher with a fully-automatic assault rifle. In some designs clips could be disposed through pump action.

The application to perpetual motion is the principle of combining multiple parts in an integrated way, specifically a way in which space is given to each feature included in the design. Additionally, efficiency is an important factor, thus, part of the principle of multiple features is to streamline the weight profile of each element included in the final package.

Systems Theory

(2) CIWS: Close-In Weapon System: This is another efficient-in-principle concept, although I did not influence its design. It is deployed on aircraft carriers as a standing defense against incoming military aircraft. It takes the form of an automated Gatling-type gun (sometimes mistakenly called by the broader name 'chain guns') attached to a large armored drum of ammunition.

The application to perpetual motion is the principle that a central design should focus on one or more primary features (e.g. like aerial defense or shooting), and other features support this role in a way that can be carefully controlled. Working from primary functions to secondary functions, to control, and back to secondary functions, and then back to primary functions becomes a way of improving strategies of engineering.

(3) Another thing to notice is the Law of Iteration observed during WWII, which is that speed of iterations often surpasses slower iterations of a slightly higher quality. In other words, processing power matters. It is always possible to overcome an obstacle,

239

given leisure and a willingness to be extreme. The exceptions are

physical impossibilities, thus, there is much advantage in the

intellectual realm, and within the range of understood knowledge.

It also amounts to a rule of creativity. Ninjas understood it as the

rule of adaption.

Systems Theory

APPLIED SYSTEMS

PUBLIC WORKS

The goal of this specific writing is to consider public works as though it were extraordinary. Sometimes lazier people are over-awed by the efforts made by public works workers, and this reputation is not entirely without meaning.

First, I will illustrate several areas of public works, and then I will describe general and specific attributes which characterize the field.

Public works includes mostly recycling and garbage disposal, street-cleaning, maintaining city sewage systems, and maintaining electricity (although sometimes these functions are also privately owned). It can also include water supply regulation and storm response, as well as a variety of clerical jobs.

Public works workers are known for the amount of work they do relative to the information involved. There is a small cross-section of information, and a strong empowerment to act on the knowledge, usually through equipment such as vehicles and cleaning tools. Some of the tasks are more technical than others, but all require considerable commitment, sometimes on a part-time basis.

One of the general properties of many aspects of public works is the desire to reduce the task to a standard medium. For example, garbage and recycling bins are standardized, and consumer goods are standardized to make processing of recycling easier, and to make most common goods easily disposable. Even furniture is often easily dismantled, rather than being built of solid metal. In this way, public works has an influence on the way society works.

In some cases, the standard medium requires more or less expertise than garbage disposal. For example, control of the city water supply is over-watched by a few experts, but is otherwise more easily maintained. Electricity and sewage, however, requires a larger number of hands-on experts, particularly when

Systems Theory

storms or heavy rains threaten the system's functioning.

Municipal staff such as electricians and sewage workers are carefully watched by city officials to make sure their work is being done effectively, and in a cost-effective manner. Annual or monthly reports are sent to office workers who are held accountable by the city government.

APPLIED SYSTEMS

VISUAL PARSING

TEXTURE CULTURE

Various textures can be used as inflection-points for new

theories. For example, a simulated landscape can be given more

texture when it has more significance. The texture can then be

preserved in compact format in relation to such-and-such figures,

with such-and-such associational symbols, etc. The recall of

corresponding landscape patterns (or whatever else) then recalls

the particular symbolic modality.

Such a usage is multi-inflective. That is, defining the logic can

affect the landscape, and defining the landscape can affect the

logic. Thus, for corresponding modalities defined such that the

landscape is affected or such that the symbols are affected, work

both ways, to create fixed landscapes or symbols, or else

open-ended landscapes or symbols determined by a query

structure. The extent of determining the symbols and landscape

244

logically will also determine the complexity and the completeness of the landscape (and to a lesser extent the symbols) simultaneously. Thus, working with a complete symbology should result in a compete landscape, and vice versa.

Another method is to use textures logically as critical reference points, which can also integrate with concept of environment. This can be expressed in terms of three primary categories: 1. Bases, 2. Extensions, and 3. Inspirations. For example, basic tessellations in 2-d and 3-d could be used as bases. Extensions would determine what type of perspective was adopted, or the types of oppositions are present on the now more realistic landscape, such as cities and gardens, or contruction and destruction, or the numbers of animals or plants, or the size and number of plants and animals or cities or gardens, etc. The focus of this would be initially compositional, but it would ultimately be defined by the 3rd card, 'inspirations' which would be like icons or focal points for the entire scene, or ethical elements like good versus evil, or category sets like 'The Elements', or sometimes textures applied to the entire landscape.

245

In my own sense of the system, a frequent focal point of the logic is the card called 'lightning covered', which simply means adding more intelligence and conceptual 'diagonalization'. For example, something that is complete can have a cycle. Something that is perfect can be paradoxical. Something that is beautiful can be multiple. Something that is wise can be powerful. Something that is mathematical can be conditional.

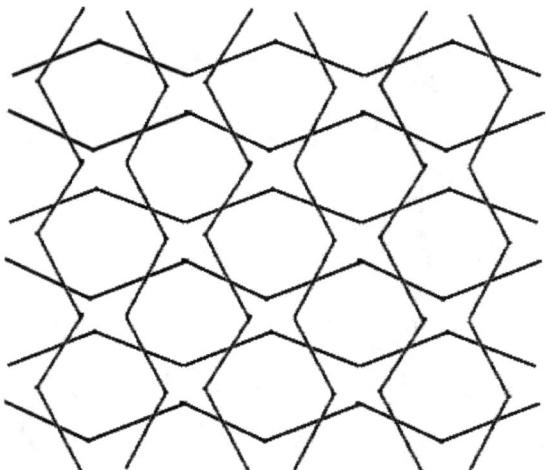

Systems Theory

APPLIED SYSTEMS

VOLITIONAL MECHANICS

Volitional mechanics has four stages, which are each part of the cycle of a perpetual motion machine

Volition - Volition is represented by the highest point of motion for the most mobile units, and the application of mass and / or momentum that happens afterwards. It expresses the machine's potential energy and general energy principle.

Devescension - This period shows the machine's ability to recover some portion of its motion automatically. It typically involves transport by downward-sloping ramps, which mirror other upwards or downwards sloping ramps.

Devolition - This incorporates both the period of devescension and the period of vescension. It may be used as a name for

the strategy of returning to a high altitude.

Vescension - During this period, which may be a long, rising,

mostly horizontal motion, the device attempts to recover

the remainder of its energy by gaining momentum.

In devices incorporating the four periods as above, it may be

observed that such devices make use of the following equations:

Hypothetical Volitional Energy =

Mobile Units / Dual-Axial Units

Hypothetical Volitional Equilibrium =

Mod. Units / (Stems Per Cycle / Sub-Cycles Per Cycle)

Volitional Efficiency or Relative Unity Rating =

Volitional Energy / Volitional Equilibrium

Systems Theory

In general, there are two requirements:

      1. Motion from rest at no cost, and

      2. Extractable energy.

And the general principle is something like,

      "Momentum without inherent velocity".

APPLIED SYSTEMS

QUALIFACTICS

A development of qualifics.

Qualifics is the science of qualities.

Qualifactics is the application of the science of qualities to fields like medicine and engineering.

Specifically, it is the ability to evoke a particular empirical pattern through qualities, such as visual and textual descriptions.

The descriptions can then be used as logical atoms of the existence of the larger state-of-affairs.

Some of these states of affairs are positive, some are negative, and some are neutral, semantic, logical, systematic, existential, etc.

Systems Theory

NEGATIVE QUALIFACTICS:

In the case of negatives, the role of qualifactics is to diagnose the problem.

When the empirical facts relating to the qualifact (description) are present, then this means that if the term is negative, a problem remains.

Removing the relevance of the qualifact has the effect of removing at least some aspect of the problem.

In the case of negative qualifacts, one of the major tools is Denial.

Denying the properties of the qualifact will have the effect of simplifying how to eliminate the overall, more specific problem which relates or depends upon the qualifact.

The use of qualifacts can be analogized with experimental science.

In this case, the CONTROL is the body of theory about the existence of a problem, including NULL HYPOTHESIS about the relevance of a problem.

The INDEPENDENT is the set of specific properties which could hypothetically relate with the problem. This may include such things as medical or other specialized knowledge. These constitute a component of the qualifact, specifically the part that can inflect or deflect a problem.

The DEPENDENT VARIABLE is the exact arrangement of facts within the qualifact (overall fact of the problem), such that a problem is observed to emerge.

In its best applications, the set of independents is such that the emergent dependent variables are unpredictable, and thus highly qualifying of a problem.

Systems Theory

In other cases, in which the qualifact is not problematic, the qualification instead involves other major interpretations, such as efficiency, evolution, complexity, or beauty.

We might interpret inflections that relate to the subject of quadriplegics.

The expression "Grollier's Number" may be said to relate to this.

As could the expression "Eforeseed".

And, the name "Clerence Thomas" spelled with an 'e' instead of an 'a' in the first vowel of the first name.

In each case, for various historical or psychological reasons, these expressions are what evokes quadriplegism. If these are the expressions that evoke quadriplegism, then either the intuition is wrong, or these are the things that signify that disease or disability.

Although this type of study might have a reputation for superstition, the emphasis is on pruning out the very best examples of trivial-or-better relation. The best examples look psychic, but in fact they rest on a firm foundation of knowledge. One of the evidences for this is that qualifactics does not depend on any occult systems like horoscopes or numerology.

It is important to keep in mind that specific qualifact statements may have multiple contingencies of assessment, meaning that just because it makes sense in one set of formal assumptions does not mean that its importance is universal.

Specifically, negative qualifactics may be seen as relating to symptomology specifically (such as its historical importance as influencing is chance of emersion), rather than the definable character of the phenomenon itself. Instead, the phenomenon itself is delegated by conventional medical prognosis, psychology, biology, etc.

Systems Theory

Thus, the tool is really a highly specialized addition to a variety of disciplines dealing with such subjects as prognosis, assessment, standards, and development.

APPLIED SYSTEMS

SEMAPHORES

Movie directing is so full of elements which follow the following process:

1. A specific direction is desired.

2. The direction is symbolized.

3. A specific symbol becomes especially conductive.

4. The conduction of the symbol places a restraint on the sum of all symbols.

For example, in philosophy (which also uses logic of some type), the symbol "<--" can be used to represent deontology, if deontology is seen as the science of a posteriori reasoning.

The symbol "<--" then becomes a theatre direction for the ultimate process of the film of play, represented also by anti-strophe.

Systems Theory

Similarly, the symbol "||" which represents pause in video recording, can be used in theatre direction to represent beginning and end-points within theatre direction.

The general pattern is that any symbol adept to signifying something for the human senses, and for rational behavior, can also be applied to the theatre.

The theatre then becomes the general constructor of semaphores.

APPLIED SYSTEMS

INFLECTICS / INFLECTIONISM

In certain cases the marks made in relation to a preexisting field will have a particular formal character, for example in music notation, or in editorial marks upon a line graph.

Marks such as the following have a prescribed significance:

/.../ Representing a break in a continuous pattern of data.

" "   " "   Repetition of previous lines or data.

Grace notes suggesting a particular musical or logical interpretation. It is these types of notations that are meant by inflection.

The science of all such intermediate yet applied symbols may be called inflectics.

Systems Theory

APPLIED SYSTEMS

KINETIC METAPHOR

This domain has not officially been named, but it is distinguished from kinesthesia, which refers to kinetic feedback or physical controls (related to haptics and ergonomics).

This term I am using to refer to a unique concept similar to kinetic metaphor. Its insight is that provided an unconscious resemblance between wo concepts, such as watery inner organs and a medieval moat, the concept that is more symbolic to the human mind (say, a medieval moat) carries heavier significance in determining the function of the original concept.

Critically, there are several possible responses, analogous to the Rhino & Caffeine concept of exceptions.

1. Maybe the only identification is a substance held in common between the two concepts, and the analogy reduces to a substance, which has an objective identity. 2. Maybe the first concept is more substantial, and the second concept is merely supporting information. But this depends on the idea that the first concept has a larger system of associations. 3. Maybe the relation exists as an ideal fantasy, and neither concept can be preferred over the other, but the correspondence is an epiphany or ideal judgment. 4. Finally, maybe the second concept is more substantial, but this requires that the second concept has a larger system of associations.

We can conclude that if we begin with things that are insignificant, we have huge potential for evolution, whereas if we begin with the significant things, the reality becomes the fantasy. This is a general observation that seems to hold even outside of kinetic metaphor.

Nathan Coppedge

APPLIED SYSTEMS

BRAIN REPAIR

"POODLE EFFECT"

This is something I have noticed that is very important, so I will mention it first. People are often set off course by the appearance of poodles! Seriously! They think their brain is composed like a poodle, and then they have to undo the effect! Until they learn to squash in these exaggerated 'puffs' of their brain, there is no hope of recovering mental function. This effect is even more extreme on the brain than the hyper-activity resulting from sugar, only the effect is opposite.

Overcoming the poodle effect could almost be called the first stage towards mental functionality. But we should ultimately avoid expressions like 'ascendent brain' as these may have similar effects, albeit not as extreme as the poodle. I have cured at least one person's thoughtlessness by mentioning this problem!

IGNORANCE-DENIAL ——Are you imagining the obvious when you need to? Are your eyes black and you have never thought they could be like charcoal, even in passing? This may be a sign of excessive mental restraint. Instead, consider the obvious, and reject it if you like. The process can be oft-repeated.

DO SOMETHING FOR YOU —- If you want appearances to 'do something for you,' this is the attitude of schizophrenia.

Systems Theory

APPLIED SYSTEMS

CHOICE SELECTION THEORY

What one should choose depends on what is optimal.(1) Should it be the thing that is most probable? This might serve the purpose of making the selection easier, or creating greater compatibility between the past and the future.

(2) Should the choice be highly selective? This might be important if it is a choice between sugar and poison. Perhaps the choice requires knowledge of some special information.

(3) Should the choice be free-willed? If what matters is one's freedom to make selections in general, than free will might be important. Maybe the best selections in general are only made if one has a habit of free willed choice.

(4) Should the choice be rational? Maybe what authenticates a choice is one's capacity for reason. In this case, the choice does not even count if it is not a rational choice. Maybe rational choices are more real than other types of choices. Or maybe reason is required for making conscious choices, if consciousness is something desirable.

(5) Should the choice be ethical? Adding ethical considerations might belabor the choice, but it might serve the advantage of assisting in determining which choices are best in the long run.

APPLIED SYSTEMS

ACTIVE PROCESS

Some cases are effective because of a constant. But in many other cases, a case may only be effective when it is "active'". This distinction between active and passive processes often defines the origin of a function. The origin of any function is in the active case.

For example, someone with 'active' biological functions in the mouth, such as a special natural acid that spurts to prevent elongated teeth, is closer to the origin of the authentic mouth.

Likewise, philosophy that is merely academic is less active than the original philosophy of the early Greek physiologoi (physical logicians), because it is the original philosophy that is more authentic for the philosophical process.

These cases seem like magic by comparison to the passive cases, and yet they are cases that do exist. In fact, these cases (including many other similar examples) define the majority of actual functions within the body, and may differ markedly from passive-functioning variations.

Systems Theory

APPLIED SYSTEMS

INTELLIGENCE ANALYSIS

This is a generic concept of "intelligence analysis" or intelligent analysis.

Step one: Find a correlated variable. For example, addiction.

Step two: Apply the variable to a network. For example, a large population may be highly affected by addiction. It may result in organized crime, a need for policing, etc.

Step three: In a specific case, find out whether the variable has relevance. This may be done for example, with the idea of risky behavior. How likely is it that someone engages in risky behavior? How likely is it that the correlated variable is interacting with the individual's network? If the person might be engaging in risky behavior, then a cohort analysis says that there is such-and-such likelihood of specific risks, such as those that affect populations.

Step four: Has the individual avoided the variable in the past? Then the analysis predicts that they will continue to avoid the variable, unless they have begun to take risks.

Step five: Now, if you want to know, does a whole nation have citizens with a particular profile, cohort risk, etc.? Then if it is a significant population, then the whole nation is at risk of activities which reflect those behaviors. (Step six: Optionally, what national activities reflect large patterns of individual behavior? What national profile characteristics predict specialized national behavior? This may require intelligence investigation.)---I didn't really learn this directly: I learned it through telepathy!---

APPLIED SYSTEMS

VIRTU-ITICS

A professor might say, "I'm not interested in how linear or predictable the system is, because I believe in virtu-itics: the true virtue of the system".

And he brings up a principle from David Hume called Hume's Arrow: that no system is strictly predictable.

"The virtue of the system, then," he says "transcends prediction"

You look at him dubiously, but then he adds: "In virtu-itics, the system is more predictable if we leave out how predictable it IS, and focus on whatever is virtuous about the system."

And that is the end of the lecture.

Systems Theory

APPLIED SYSTEMS

STANDARD CRITIQUE

Basically, if different standards are held by the two theories, one must determine if the standards are compatible.

1. If the standards are not compatible but show different things, assess whether the theories are valid independently. Perhaps neither is 'true'.
2. If the standards are compatible but show different things, accept that the theories explain different aspects of the same phenomena, or even entirely separate phenomena that are part of the same standard of critique or reality.
3. If the standards are compatible and show the same thing, then determine in what way the math / language aspect is expressing the same thing. This may require large or small leaps.
If the standards are not compatible and show the same thing, it is time to widen the range of standards and theories that refer to the phenomena. It is likely that there are other aspects which have not been described which have equal importance to the existing perspectives. Collectively a new theoretical attitude would be created.

APPLIED SYSTEMS

EXCEPTIONAL REPLACEMENT THEORY

The sense, for example, in which there may be better alternatives to quantum theory with enough information.

If total probability has no proof, and total proof has no probability, the choice is to accept partial knowledge, to have a limited set of absolutes, or to reject probability or absoluteness, resulting in proof or probability.

Other cases exist where if one concept is absolute, its opposite becomes eliminated. The categories which lie outside the system: naive realism, irrationality, paradoxes, and incoherence become the common forms of absoluteness when none of the possible categories are universal.

If it is likely that a concept is not universal (perhaps as proven by the existence of more than one axis of measurement) then either the first concept or its opposite may be considered absolutely probable, as the only alternative is a choice between pure prob-ability in regards to those categories, or pure absoluteness. Thus, the system defers to the four exceptions, or becomes absolutely probable and therefore logical, or understandable in terms of pure probability or pure absoluteness. All of this can be seen as depend-ing on the judgment of the universality of a category, which can be seen as context-dependent or even paradigm-driven.

DRAMATIC

SYSTEMS

Nathan Coppedge

Systems Theory

DRAMATIC SYSTEMS

DRAMATIC LESSONS

Right: A basic image of dramatic lessons in the form of plot arcs within a story.

The typical example is that, through a distended process of dramatic resolution, a central character finds himself in the midst of trickery, illusions, or a romantic engagement.

The plot leads the character to

commit evil deeds.

A summary of the story in a more

condensed form would be that

'the protagonist's own inherent

evil leads to his downfall'.

However, there are many other

types of stories.

Stories often connect to other stories through the idea of Fate,

Free Will, Serendipity, or Good Fortune and that is what

fascinates me.

Stories are often connected by the elements that have already

been introduced.

For example, someone with money might lose money. Someone

with money more than once might have a strategy for retaining money. And the same for love, privilege, trust, etc.

Someone who is once male might become female.

Someone stupid might become a philosopher.

Someone foolish may eventually teach school.

It is these kinds of stories that bind the most intriguing elements of Fate, Free Will, Serendipity, and Good Fortune.

PSYCHO-
LOGICAL
SYSTEMS

Systems Theory

PSYCHOLOGICAL SYSTEMS

INFANTILE PSYCHOLOGY

Infants, it is known, have a lot of care for their mothers.

Much of the infant's immediate life has to do with his or her dependence on the mother.

The infant may also learn a lot from the mother's and father's response to him or her, and the initial experiences in the hospital or wherever else the infant is born.

Indeed, the child's early experiences are exaggerated. Depending on what senses are available to the child, the infant may learn considerably, or else not as much as average.

The earliest experiences are the moments in which the infant reaches the first inclinations towards whatever wisdom or insight that will be had later in life.

This first insight has two parts: (1) The child's unhindered perceptions about the world, whether pleasant or unpleasant, whether insightful, or recoiling, etc. and (2) The permission granted throughout later life to trust these perceptions and enjoy or critique existence.

The first major opportunity for the infant may be to avoid suffering, and if this is not successful the world becomes a treacherous place, full of shadows and phantoms.

The second opportunity is to be wise, and this is on the basis of the extent to which the infant's first insights can blossom. That is, whether the infant was confused or not. How fresh in memory, how free of narcotics was the mother, etc.

The third opportunity is to be critical, which is something that tends to happen to a greater extent if the child is unhappy, but also when the child is supported by the environment.

Systems Theory

Thus, the Happy, Wise, and Petulent children are the three

archetypes that emerge. And their semiforms are respetively the

Funny, Intelligent, and Perceptive.

The best to emerge from a bad life is the perceptive child, while

the best to emerge from a good life is the happy child. In that

way, there is some compensation for the pains of life.

PSYCHO-ANALYTIC SYSTEMS

MAINSTREAM PSYCHOLOGY

Mainstream psychology has a reputation for a certain nimble, affable attitude which makes its subjects more appealing to a popular audience. This form of psychology is virtually unique for its 1-to-1 relevance to the audience, and its immediate applicability in the personal and inter-personal world of its audience.

Mainstream psychology is often summarized in individual 'grand theses', often combining words such as 'individual (adj.)', 'passivity / aggression / intelligence / schizophrenia / depression', 'improves / spirals out of control', 'under some [stated] conditions'. The conditions can be stated to be a byproduct of further factors such as 'de-socialization / de-sensitization / stimulation / group settings'. Some bizarre theses seem to hold under the conditions of certain illnesses, or under bizarre stimulus. Thus, some of the conditions may have results only under 'over-exposure / with high intensity' or 'if the client is sensitive to the stimulus'.

Systems Theory

Thus, mainstream psychology can be mapped as follows:

1. Sensitive?

2. Exposed?

3. Bizarre?

4. Social psychology?

5. Stimulus? De-sensitized or de-socialized?

6. Condition?

7. Chronic?

8. Depressed?

9. Dysfunctional?

10. Intelligent (specific sensitivity)?

11. Passive / aggressive (hidden symptoms)?

For example,

A. Bee-sting. Physical sensitivity. Requires physical treatment or tolerance.

B. Allergy to yogurt. Sensitivity with a condition. May affect certain social situations.

C. Person is behaving bizarrely because they are not wearing any clothes. Person may have dementia or excessive promiscuity. Problem needs to be solved immediately.

D. Person feels social anxiety. Person is otherwise mentally healthy. Condition which applies in all social situations.

E. Person has a concealed megalomania. This is social psychology that applies only in certain social situations.

F. Person is feeling discomfort in the office. This may be a product of a physical or mental condition.

G. Person is feeling very alert. The person may be drugged or experiencing psychosis or exaggerated emotions.

H. Person doesn't show up at the appointment. Person may be dis-organized, forgetful, or have a physical impairment.

I. Person's condition doesn't improve. The condition may be habit-ual, chronic, fatal, or in some other way serious.

J. Person is dysfunctional and blames their mood. Person may be depressed.

Systems Theory

K. Person doesn't handle social situations very well. Person may

be emotionally immature, abused, schizophrenic, or developmentally abnormal (high I.Q.).

L. Person is especially complex on one issue. Person may simply

have special knowledge in this area (high I.Q.).

M. Person is especially un-forthcoming on one particular topic in her life. Person may have suppressed memories.

PSYCHO-ANALYTIC SYSTEMS

HARMONIZING

There is much confusion about the concept of harmonization. It has been seen as central to functional psychology for a long time. However, its root causes, and the means of sustaining it have been (for some) by turns difficult or obscure.

Harmonizing, which is the process of reaching harmonization, comes about through a practical focus on positive thinking, both to avoid disaster, and to promote valuable mentalistic vibes.

Harmonization becomes more difficult for those who are brain-damaged, or for some other reason cannot find genuine mental stimulation. The ability to stimulate the mind is what separates so-called 'ordinary' people from those who are considered abnormal. Further traits such as ethical conduct, professional qualifications, fatherliness or motherliness, etc. seperate further the functional types, but for dysfunctional people some or all of these additional traits may often be impossible.

Harmonization becomes the exclusive bridge between functional and dysfunctional people, and it is by no means an easy bridge to cross, as the positive elements of harmony are held almost exclusively by functional people.

A key element to understand is that harmonizing involves ignoring and eliminating harmful vibes, which can be detected and criticized by those with intellectual sensitivity. The truly functional people tend to be high intellectual performers, or at least high social performers.

On the converse, ignoring harmful vibes has been critiqued as a 'following-the-herd' mentality, but so long as mental stimulation is a desirable end in itself, some degree of conformism is largely unavoidable, and can even inspire envy.

Intellectual sensitivity and higher cognitive traits become the defense against invasive negative behaviors that could compromise the culture and chemistry of such close-knit networks of reward and response.

The reward, some say it is a lofty one, is to be mentally constructive by providing a culture for the higher mental ambitions of groups of individuals. Because groups tend to have higher social functions than individuals, there is an advantage in giving preference to group function over individual function.

On the other hand, ignoring individual function may prohibit creativity if the focus is no longer on genuine individual accomplishment. Thus, the model must be accepted on a chemical level of mutual exchange before harmonization works for individuals.

It is then likely that the system of harmonization is keyed into patterns that only emerge with sexual or narcotic stimulus.

So, while harmony works for society, it is superficial in the sense that it has no one individual's interest in mind independent of the overall social function.

On the other hand, it is geared towards the immediate chemical achievement of every individual in the context of any existing context of limitations.

Harmony thus involves such things as simple awareness, the desire for stimulus, and social priorities which are assumed to be the honest traits of humans as individuals when they seek to fulfill non-negativist priorities.

PSYCHO-ANALYTIC SYSTEMS

INDIVIDUATION

INSPIRATION --- At first, the individual (subject) is surrounded by talented people, often people who play music instruments. Their talent is explained by the fact that they have already individuated. This is also the time when the person first hears the word 'individual'.

THE LIE --- The person sees that there is something wrong with the world. The person struggles and is taken down by a psychological or physical condition of some type. He or she hears the word 'individuation' if it is psychological, or 'habit' / 'habitation' / 'habituation' if it is physical. The physical response leads to questions such as, is it worth it to spend time, is life worth it, is the physical world inspiring, etc. It cannot be argued that both worlds are equally interesting, so the physical answer may involve some sort of artificial death or historical lapse into the psychological condition. In effect, the physical model becomes the

286

background.

THEORY AND PROOF --- The individual explores creativity or whatever else he or she feels like doing. The result is a theory (what he or she is doing) and confirmation (proof of the theory), not to be confused with the later stage.

IMMERSION OR DENIAL ---- As life becomes more like a mental construct that responds to some of the person's thoughts (e.g. the person gets some of what is wanted), either the person immerses him or herself in pleasures, or he or she denies him or herself some of the pleasures. The result is two different personalities, one finding unreality in the physical body, and the other finding unreality in the mind.

CONFORMATION --- The theory, whether it is flesh or mind, becomes all-important, and the persons' beliefs as they become more sophisticated are also confirmed or supported.

ELEVATION - THE KISS ---- Rewards become immaterial or else confirm one's habituation in the world. One enters 'the psychological cocoon'.

PSYCHO-ANALYTIC SYSTEMS

GESTALT THEORY

Take a value and find out that it's true, and theoretically you've found what is known as a 'gestalt' or deep psychological truism.

For example, if authentic life is happy, and happiness is always symbolized by the color 'yellow', then we can say 'life is yellow' is a gestalt. Even if it isn't 100% true, it is a truism because its supposed to be true.

Similarly, we can say 'systems live in trees' if all systems come from linear structures which are called trees.

Systems Theory

PSYCHO-ANALYTIC SYSTEMS

MNEMOSIS

Mnemosis, or recovery of memories, is a technique that has fallen out of fashion in psychology. Psychologists have discovered that patients are dishonest, temperamental, or just can't get themselves to remember everything.

Nonetheless, confrontation with past events is an important process in therapy, and takes place even if it is not frankly acknowledged. And, often the therapist is aware of this.

The process may vary somewhat, but it is usually in the following form:

1. The therapist asks the patient polite questions (how he or she is feeling, what is something that matters to them, where have they traveled to, etc.)

2. The therapist asks the patient to explain something in their life

that is important to them, such as a memory that they think of fondly, or some recent experience that has troubled them.

3. Instead of immediately analyzing what the trouble or significance means, the therapist asks the person what the thing, event, significance, etc. means to the patient.

4. Through internally analyzing what the patient interprets from the experience, the therapist begins to understand the patient.

5. The therapist can develop a network of associations about the patient by asking more questions, and delving deeper into the patient's past experiences and associations.

6. Finally, through guidance from the therapist, the patient is led into an understanding of what is most important to them.

7. If what seems most important is something harmful or dangerous, the therapist can warn the patient that there is something harmful or dangerous lurking in their psyche.

Systems Theory

PSYCHO-ANALYTIC SYSTEMS

EPOCTICS

This is a formal domain lying between logic and applied theory.

It is the study of formal properties emerging from the relation of

base to height to shape to impression.

It may be seen as part of the psychology of aesthetics.

The shape of a thing is considered flexible, while the base and the

height are considered to be the functors of theory.

The feeling or impression of the thing depends on the shape.

So, for example,

(A) Too Subtle **(B) Just Right** **(C) Un-Attainable**

In this figure,

Very small shapes of a certain type may be 'too subtle' e.g. too subtle to perceive or comprehend, or make an impression.

At a particular size, the shapes begin to add up to make impressions. The overall impression, however, is often one of multiple shapes combined into one shape. Thus, the big shape (C) is unattainable: it is really a composite of smaller shapes.

One way to view Epoctics is that it is the science of the hierarchy of shapes. But it is really more specialized than that. Epoctics sees shapes in terms of dots, and may relate through Gestalt

Systems Theory

theory to concepts of completeness and compositionality.

Through the importance of Gestalt theory, it becomes a domain of

psychology, and also through its insistence on measurable

aesthetic properties.

Nathan Coppedge

PHENOMENO-

LOGICAL

SYSTEMS

Systems Theory

PHENOMENOLOGICAL SYSTEMS

PHENOMENOLOGY

Stage 1:

Select a word that represents your concept of reality.

Stage 2A:

Prune out what is not a good experience. Express the bad

concepts as separate systems if it is desirable to develop them.

Gradually reject the bad ideas.

Stage 2B:

Experience the ideal modalities of the concept. For example,

excitement, beauty, epiphany, and transcendence.

Stage 3A:

Explore the phenomenal world as you have discovered it, and

simultaneously explore the life of the modalities. Develop

principles of modality.

Stage 3B

If a concept does not have life, creatively modify it, or explore

dynamic modalities using the principles of modality

earlier-discovered.

Stage 4:

Return to your initial concept, and modify it as necessary.

Repeat stages 1 - 4 as necessary.

Optional Stage 5:

Explore the experience of phenomenal knowledge. Introduce new

theories of critique. Examine your life.

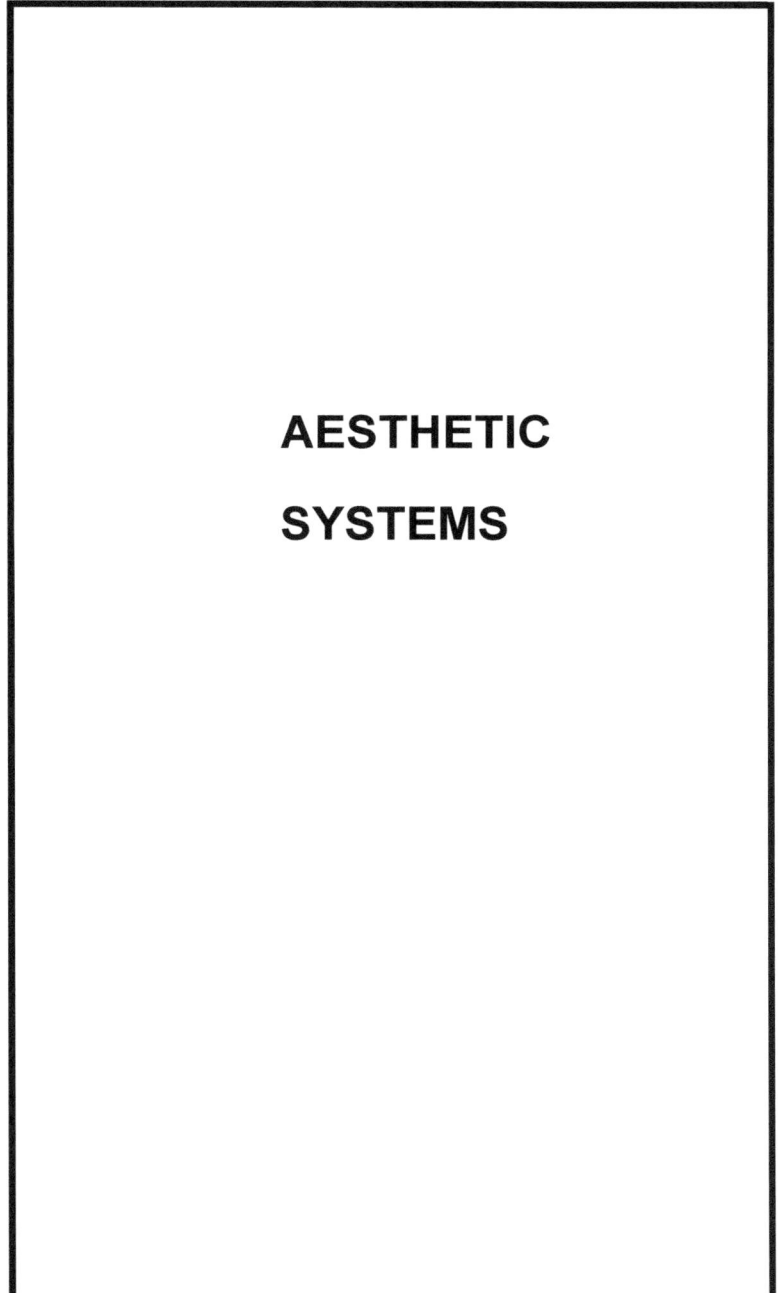

AESTHETIC

SYSTEMS

Nathan Coppedge

300

AESTHETIC SYSTEMS

ARCHETYPAL AESTHETICS

RULES OF ARCHETYPAL AESTHETICS

What can be incidentally beautiful can be conceptual.

What can be conceptualized can compose a logic.

What can be formalized as by logic can be improved into archetype.

What is archetypal may be compared to ultimate beauty.

AESTHETIC SYSTEMS

HYPER-LANDSCAPES

This is called a system, because it is the intellectualization of fantasy landscapes. It has its roots in Zen, but recently has played a large role in defining the deeper meaning of science fiction. Nonetheless, it is a discipline that is often overlooked. Some writers assume that it belongs only to the medieval, i.e. 'the land of the fairies' (a childhood feeling), or to a particular epoch, such as commonly the Renaissance, or feudal Japan. However, in reality, the tools of intellectualizing fantasy landscape are more broad and general than any specific period. They are even more general than science fiction. And, they are often employed in the best fantasy games.

Abyssthmus : An island in the middle of an abyss, represents the ultimate magical or natural achievement. Yet it is often called for-saken' suggesting that it takes a long time to get there. Sometimes the island is never reached. It becomes a romantic ideal. The yin-yang: possibility within impossibility. The positive principle.

Takeover Aesthetic: In games like Mario Bros. a single aesthetic takes over, suggesting (1) The influence of a mastermind, such as someone who would create logic puzzles, and (2) The exaggerated appropriateness of variation within the scheme.

Magic Paper: Contains the key to all power, so long as it doesn't catch fire. The power of fate. Also, microcosm within macrocosm.Destruction: Scattered remnants of puzzles, machines, cities, items, etc. provides an opportunity to reflect on all that it meant. However, what a waste! Unless the stuff springs back! Ultimately destruction is just an aesthetic, or a sign of industry.

Enchantments: Powerful enchantments give the deceptive appearance of reality. Sometimes the illusion only appears during certain times of day. The wizards must be proud, but everyone else must remain wary! Enchantment is similar to virtual reality and hallucination, somewhat analogous to sophistry and artistic inspiration.

Qualified Nature: Somewhat analogous to the Takeover Aesthetic, qualified nature is when nature has special attributes like unicorns, aqua vitae, or Heaven. Granting nature these attributes is often the last chance for their possibility. The magical attributes are governed by specialized laws involved in the fates of mortals, to prevent damages.

Special Abilities: Powers like time travel, immortality, teleportation, and invisibility connect the landscape with higher dimensions, such as immortal time, alternate universes, time eddies, and metaphysics.

Equipped with knowledge of some of these things, the explorer ventures out, discovering new aesthetic puzzles, each of them solved when it is understood.

AESTHETIC SYSTEMS

GAME AESTHETICS

From the time of Ancient Egypt and the Greek Arcades, and perhaps earlier, there have been many designs for games, particularly board games, nimble games, group games, and private games, amongst others.

Games often feature minor characteristics from mathematics and social or political comprehension, particularly winning and losing and the resulting (sometimes pretend) difference in social status.

Lying and fighting were early examples of games which are now taken very seriously, and sometimes punished. Justice itself was once seen as a kind of 'game of the gods', associated with concepts such as Hubris (offending the gods) and Moira (the influence of one Fate over another).

In the game of chess we see an aesthetic of competing identical social orders. Some would argue that the aesthetics of chess is very different from its strategy.

In games such as Mancala and Cribbage players are asked to make basic strategic decisions involving numbers or combinations of cards.

Games have played an important role in defining the abstractions which lie behind religious, mythological, and metaphysical concepts.

At one time games may have been considered magical, but now they are often treated as toys for mathematical and social education.

To some extent the strongest component of games has always been the beliefs of those teaching them. Exaggeration, doubt, and epiphany have been important elements of games for a long time.

If I focus on board games in particular, the aesthetic of games involves such things as:

1. Pieces, beads, etc.

2. Categories, holes, etc.

3. Designs, etc.

4. Rules, options, etc.

5. Strategies, concepts, etc.

So, in general, the intensity of a board game is derived by an exponential relationship placing concepts first and pieces last. The most adaptable element of a board game appears to be the board itself, followed by the aesthetic of the board, and the rules used to play on the board. The strategies and ways the pieces are used are the least flexible elements.

Systems Theory

IMPOSSIBLE PROBLEMS

Some problems seem too difficult to solve. Therefore, it becomes necessary to visualize the puzzle before reaching a solution. Visualization offers the benefit of abbreviating all the logical symbols.

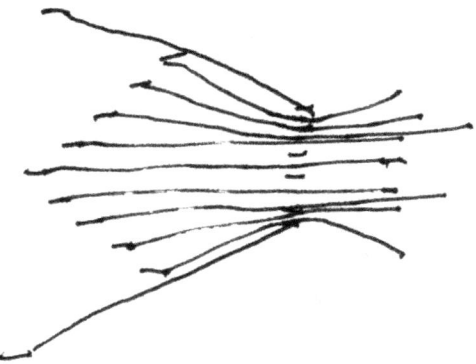

Pictured is a sign called 'The cuirass of the amazon'. It is a result of just such a logical conundrum. Generalizing from the solution to this puzzle (since it is really the cuirass of Athena), we reach a general methodology for many impossible puzzles:

1. Try lateral thinking.

2. Reverse the logic.

3. Apply higher logic.

4. 4. Connect the dots.

5. 5. If all else fails, try again.

AESTHETIC SYSTEMS

THE METAPHYSICAL ART

Metaphysical Levels of the 3rd Dimension According to Aestheticu-reanism or Asceticureanism The metaphysical art is the art of changeless variations. Here are motions within the art:

(A) There are two boulders of equal size. Place an equally-sized boulder between them.

(B) There is a small boulder and a very large boulder. Place a medium-sized boulder between them.

(C) There is a small boulder and a very large boulder. Imagine an infinite boulder beyond the large boulder.

(D) There is a small boulder and a very large boulder. Find something small and magical in the sand beyond the smaller boulder. If you do not find something, do your best to put something small and magical there in place of the missing object. If you return later, take the object, or return the object, creating a

308

Systems Theory

cycle of nature.

(E) Swing a cheap object on a string, to advertise the one small magical object that you do not possess, or the infinite ones that you do, but which may be invisible.

(F) Make compositions out of precious objects, finding magic in them. Think if you must.

(G) Try to balance something on a tall pole stuck in the ground. If you cannot balance the object, then become a tragedian by worshipping the invisible things on the end of the protruding stick.

(H) Pretend you are a victim to lament the possible loss of immortality. Stick sticks in the ground and lie on your back underneath the sticks, like you have been impaled by the invisible. Construct a spirit to equal the ghosts on the ends of the poles.

(I) Carry a stick to keep in touch with the ghosts in things.

Become animated with the way of the world.

(J) Put a precious magical thing on a string around your neck. Now you don't need to play victim. Give it a name, like 'wishing stone' or 'philosopher's stone' or 'washing-stone' or 'stone of youth'.

(K) If you don't like the stone, throw it in the water. When you feel thoughtful, look for a replacement stone. If you love the stone, keep it on a shelf. Become a hermit.

(L) Ruminate, so that you remember just how things are.

(M) Practice un-attachment, and learn time-travel.

At this point, if you succeed, you have mastered metaphysics for three dimensions.

From the forthcoming *Dimensional Metaphysics Toolkit*.

SENSE SYSTEMS

Nathan Coppedge

Systems Theory

SENSE SYSTEMS

THE 5 SENSES

Sense | Sense organ

Sight   Eyes

Touch   Primarily fingers

Taste   Tongue

Smell   Nose and olfactory glands

Hearing   Ear drums and ears

SENSE SYSTEMS

THE SIXTH SENSE

FORMS OF PSYCHIC PREDICTION

Psychic prediction may take several basic forms.

First I will describe the most basic types of prediction.

First of all, the most basic type is 0-dimensional prediction. This consists of predicting what has already occurred, that is, predicting the types of things that have already happened. A second degree of this is had by predicting things that are similar to those things that have happened. For our purposes, this can be called simple generalization. If Henrick usually wants to play games, perhaps he wants to play games now. This is the first dimension of prediction, and it is the type that gains most easily by probabilistic inductions. This method is also called specialized prediction when it is applied to specialized modes of behavior. For example, we can predict that a Matisse will sell high compared to an unknown artist. We know that popular items in an auction sell high, whereas unpopular items might not sell at all. Therefore,

there is an exponential relationship for example, between selling

a Matisse, and selling a Matisse at an auction. These kinds of

things can be predicted by studying the specific character of the

modalities and events involved in a given situation. However, if

an event is instead informal or contrived, this lends an aspect of

unpredictability. The predictions only work when all of the prior

conditions are met, and become less predictable with every

difference from the previous cases. Therefore, differences can be

used to predict differences, as another type of specialized

prediction. It may help to predict trickery or confusion ('likely

outcomes'), rather than predicting a specific event. It should be

accepted that some conditions and choices are arbitrary. Because

we do not know if conditions will be met to satisfaction, we know

that some events are arbitrary. If the conditions are one half

different, then prediction requires a strong degree of formalism,

however that is calculated. It involves, in effect, exceeding

expectations, or coming across an event that happened just in the

same way, but as if by chance. This is one reason that scientists

have been known to require the reproduction of laboratory

conditions, even with highly predictable phenomena. Thus, specialized predictions have some limitations.

The next type is delineative or elaborative prediction. What it consists of is a generalization modified by additional imagination about the significance of the factors involved. This type of prediction can be called variablistic, because it often functions by applying a generalization to a deduction about a variable. If elephants are painted red, perhaps it is a sight for sore eyes, etc. One form of this is prediction through emergence. This is not necessarily a linear prediction because it essentially doesn't predict based on existing data. Nor does it predict based on known exterior data. Instead, it involves a conclusion that something is missing from the data. Logical conclusions are drawn so that we can make major systemic conclusions about what the data means. The new theory appears as if from thin air. This is similar to the emergence of Darwinism, or the genetic explanation of reproduction. What determines the success of these theories is their relative importance, not necessarily the lack of any alternative. It is the importance of the theory----its emergence----which drives the prediction. (Many theories from social science involve emergent theories, such as socialism and capitalism. Instead of acting as a formal constraint, they often expand the way that the conditions function. In this case, the explanation is not erroneous, but instead, serves as a new rational mode of explanation).

A third type is contingent or categorical prediction. If something is the case, then we can predict that the things that rely upon this first condition are modified when that category is modified. This form of prediction works better for predicting quality differences than actually-different conditions. However, if multiple qualities are absent, predictions can be made about the alternatives. If there is no snow, it can be predicted that it is not cold, or there is a shortage of water, for instance. If it is not cold, one can predict that it is arid or moist. If there is a shortage of water, one can predict that it is dry, or there is a high tolerance for water. This can also take the form of complex categorization. Attaching variables to a given object means that predicting the outcome for the main object affects the outcome of some, if not all, of the variables. For example, 'if we do something extreme, the change might be observable. Otherwise, it is an abstract or un-measurable form of extremity. We must have some means of observation, or we can usually conclude that the effects are not extreme. Or we can adopt an irrational view'.

A fourth type of prediction is coherent prediction. This is also called synergism or epiphany. The simplest form of coherent prediction occurs by the exclusion of all but one unlikely option. Hella spent a hot day in the desert, and she was outdoors, and walked several miles, time passed and she didn't expire: she must have brought something to drink with her. A more complex form occurs by qualifying what it means to make a given combination. People who have complicit sex are always lovers. Therefore, if two people have sex, it might be complicit, and they might be lovers. Or, something is complicit between two people. If it is sex, they are lovers. This can even involve highly complex phenomena. For example: Joe defines himself as an editor, but he works as an economist. In some way he is doing economic editing. This is the beginning of a genuinely psychic method. Attaching judgments of fully embraced variables can be a meaningful way of

reaching for epiphanies. For example, what 'definitely IS

something' about a given thing? Then apply that condition to

factors like responsibility, organization, and predictability. An

exception to this is so-called 'black swans'. In that case, one must

predict the rationale which makes something a black swan. The

rule in that case is that things are either unreasonable,

reasonable, without purpose, or serving a prescribed function. A

method for solving black swans involves corroboration or

defaulting. This occurs when there is no better explanation

remaining for a given thing. Well, we know that such-and-such a

creature has eyes based on the related species, but nothing about

the creature looks exactly like eyes. The eyes must be these

spots on its back. Otherwise its blind. Or, black swans could exist,

as long as we know that color serves no inherent function.

Now for more genuine psychic predictions:

A second genuine form of psychic prediction involves using a

posteriori reasoning on a 0-dimensional prediction. For example, if we know that some events are arbitrary, then we can derive

that we don't know if some conditions will be met to satisfaction.

If we know Henrick wants to play games now, we can predict that

he usually wants to play games. This form of prediction often

involves deducing the types of statements that lead to a particular

line of reasoning: that is, predicting a rationale. Many psychics

are familiar with this way of phrasing deductions.

A third form of genuine psychic prediction involves determination

based on unstated facts. Since everyone thinks about the

opposite of what they say, at least unconsciously, combining

multiple opposite terms for terms that have been stated as

someone's opinion, or as the definition of a motive or interest for

the person or organization, will give information about the

genuine motivations, or else the looming unknowns in the life of

the person or organization. For example, if someone states that

the first thing on their mind is their motorcycle, and the second

thing on their mind is their manhood, then you can predict that

they're concerned about meeting someone else on a motorcycle.

Systems Theory

A fourth form of genuine psychic prediction involves categorical relationships. One can ask or predict 'what is someone's usual mode of relation with the world?' Then one can predict that they use that mode of relation with their perceived opposites. For example, an artist who expresses that the thing on his mind is cars can be predicted 'not to buy a painting of a car, instead you'll make it yourself' (the concealed opposition is between the artist who makes art, and his opposite, the buyer of the art. The opposite of making a painting of a car is buying a painting of a car). Similarly, if a business expresses itself as aggressive and competitive, but you think they're liars, you can predict they'll have contradictory marketing ('competing truths', since their mode of relation is competition, and their opposite is the truth).

A fifth form of genuine psychic prediction: take any number of factors describing a current event or situation you're in, and reverse the factors that are different from the subject. This can be used to predict how someone is feeling, or what their core motivation are. For example, an artist is at a business convention. So they're feeling unconventional, and they feel like making art, since that is not a different motive from business. Or, a

philosophy society is at an art gallery. So, it thinks its popular art

('society' does not conflict with 'gallery'), and it thinks its un-

philosophical art, or tries to make connections between art and

philosophy ('philosophy' is different from 'art' or it can be

debated). Other conclusions might be that they think art is trying

to commercialize philosophy, that philosophy ought to involve

graphics, or to view art or philosophy as a socialist movement.

Those are the eight categories of prediction that I have

determined. I hope this writing may be considered useful to my

readers on this most often unrealized subject.

Works Cited

Coppedge, Nathan. The Dimensional Psychologist's Toolkit.

CSIP, 2014

Systems Theory

SENSE SYSTEMS

TELESIS

Detecting wave functions, sensitivity to mathematical properties, specifically 'expressions' conforming to natural law variations, or telesis may be important for developing new theories of physics, mathematics, engineering, chemistry, medicine, etc.

For example, in medicine (pharmacology) there may be a requirement for sensitivity to the properties of powders. In engineering there may be a sensitivity to the micro-properties of computers, and a sensitivity to structural stress.

An obscure variation on telesis is telesis volitio (perpetual motion sensitivity) which has various forms often involving four-dimensional knowledge, as well as knowledge of friction and proportionality, and there may be other further concerns, such as the sensitivity to an invention or conceptualization, rather than an explicit formula.

SENSE SYSTEMS

INHERENT VISION

While directional vision sees objects in 3-d perspective, inherent vision is a different kind of vision in which objects are perceived as if from their own perspective, or perhaps, with some form of interpreter, or multiple, localized perspectives.

For inherent vision, the images exists inside the mind as an experience of what it is to be or to be around the object. The perception of the object has been extended away from its supposed objective location, which can now be compared to one-dimensionality, and now exists as a living thing within the mind.

If 'life' is the common element of inherent vision, then inherent vision may be compared not just to dimensional extension and complexification, but also to the desirable evolution of any object.

Systems Theory

Inherent vision becomes a platform consciousness application, that is, an application that may have special utility for higher levels of consciousness than the 3-d.

Inherent vision in the universe as we know it can be defined as a basic form of 4-d vision. But in another world where the first dimension is consciousness, inherent vision might be one fraction of a unified perception analogous to 1-d Monism.

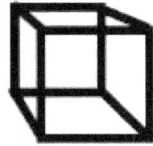

Linear Vision

**Roughly Inherent Vision
(and many other
objects simultaneosly)**

Nathan Coppedge

RUBRIC

SYSTEMS

Nathan Coppedge

Systems Theory

RUBRIC SYSTEMS

HIERARCHY OF BIOLOGY

UNIVERSES

PLANET SYSTEMS

PLANETS

ECOSYSTEMS

SOCIETIES

ORGANISMS

ORGAN SYSTEMS

ORGANS

TISSUES

CELLS

ORGANELLES

MOLECULES

ATOMS

SUB-ATOMIC PARTICLES

*

*Adapted from Miller, Harley. General Zoology Bio 100. New York: McGraw-Hill Create, 2013.

RUBRIC SYSTEMS

FUNCTIONAL HIERARCHY

Hierarchies of functions don't exist in every discipline, but when they do occur, the division can be marked.

A typical example is the business hierarchy.

Another example is the traditional division of a house shown below:

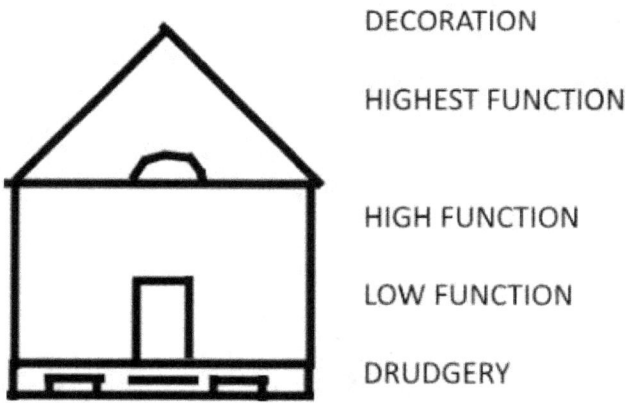

DECORATION

HIGHEST FUNCTION

HIGH FUNCTION

LOW FUNCTION

DRUDGERY

The division can be analogized to the higher and lower functions of the brain, in which higher functions typically control or man-age

lower functions, and higher functions typically serve a more

'beautified' purpose which holds greater honor and prestige in

society.

Social functions such as reproduction, possession of property and

wealth, and high-functioning jobs are typically considered to be

more prestigious and of higher rank than menial jobs, disability,

and homelessness.

Occasionally exaggerated importance is given to individuals who

gain high status from a low position. But it is more likely that such

a person would become a king than that the entire hierarchy

would be inverted.

RUBRIC SYSTEMS

FOOD PYRAMID

Eat these Last!--->

Sugar, Fat

Dairy, Milk, Cheese

Carbohydrates: Beans, Bread, Crackers

Fruits & Vegetables: Spinach, Pears, Oranges Etc.

Eat these First! --->

Systems Theory

RUBRIC SYSTEMS

QUALITY CONTROL (QC)

1 - The best quality.

|

2 - High quality.

|

3 - Room for improvement

|

4 - Average, neither good nor bad.

|

5 - Below standard, disappointing.

|

6 - Poor, questionable.

|

7 - Shoddy, very poor, dangerous.

RUBRIC SYSTEMS

EPICUREAN BODY TYPES

A Disaffected Perspective

Strong and stupid, no sense.

Medium build, with skill in a trade.

Effeminate but not gay to appease stronger men and indulge intellect.

Tall, with great intellect.

Tom-boy or lesbian. Unresolved feelings.

Self-flattering. Cares for family. Religious sentiment.

Sensuous appearance, but not passionate. Knowledge of life.

Short, with the ability to dart between rooms.

Systems Theory

RUBRIC SYSTEMS

FORMAL STANDARDS

There are a number of ways to view standards archetypally.

1-d:

Meaningful Systems

2-d:

Complexity is perfect.

Perfection is complex.

3-d:

One way to view standards is that everything is a linear structure.

Another way is that everything is cyclical, self-inferential.

Another way is that everything is an isometric projection, with

extreme standardization, and only subtle variation.

4-d:

One way is that finite things are finite, and infinite things are

infinite.

Another way is reductive, and all is one substance. There is no

complexity.

Another way is typological, and even infinity has finite complexity.

Another way is that there are infinite complexities at infinite

distance.

Systems Theory

RUBRIC SYSTEMS

HOURS OF INSPIRATION

The most exciting events happen at the earliest hour.

The clock ticks one hour longer every day.

One day later every hour.

Inspirations are by Occasion.

Create an occasion and learn the hours!

The hours are women!

The goddess is the daylight shining bright!

Time is an alien form of life!

God is from the machine!

"Swords turn to plowshares!

Crocuses turn green!"

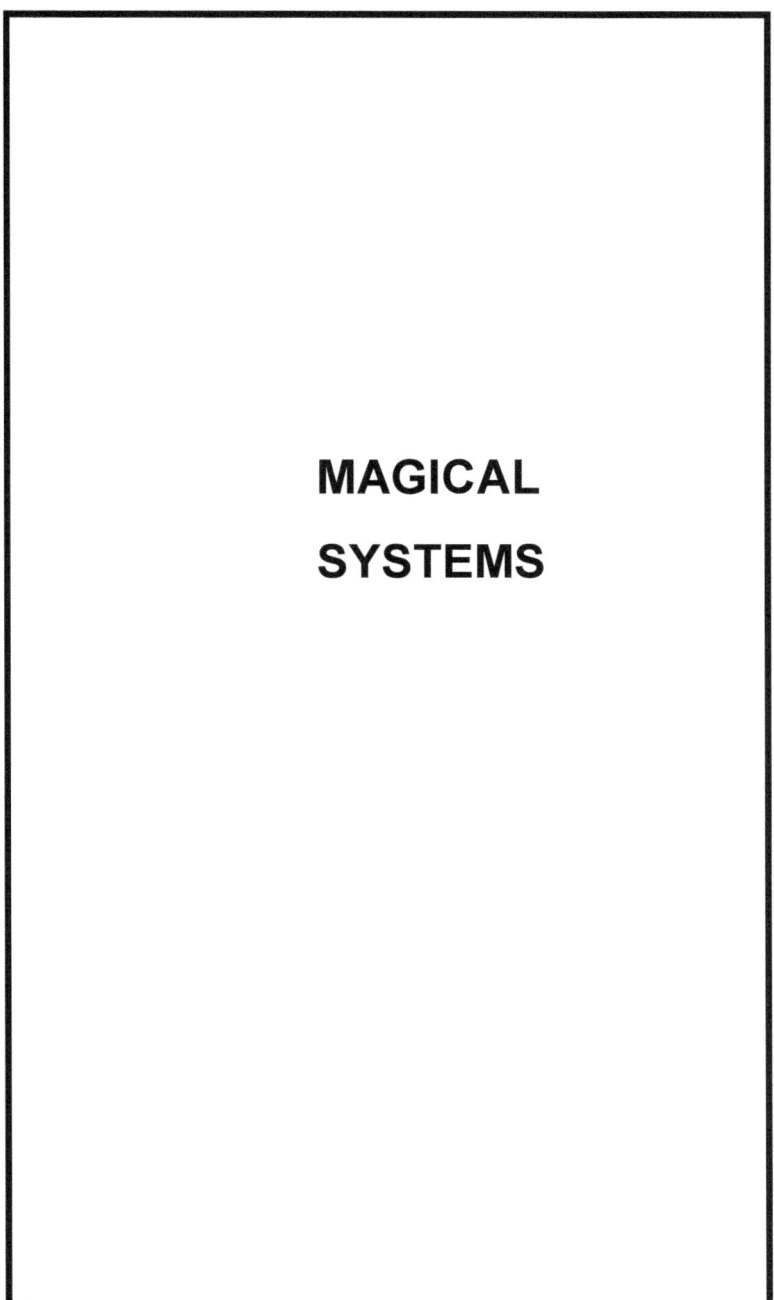

MAGICAL

SYSTEMS

Nathan Coppedge

Systems Theory

MAGICAL SYSTEMS

"KEN" OR KENNING

This is an intuitive sense of knowledge that existed during the medieval period, especially amongst 'women of the town'. Insights about similarities between elements of nature, and commonsense insights about the way of the world are combined to yield something that passes for wisdom. Unfortunately, during later periods in history, much of this basic wisdom has been lost. But one of the reasons is that it was not very universal. Its use appeared (notoriously) to depend on the intelligence of the user, and those who were not as bright frequently lost track of the (highly) 'original' meaning. At least as it came to be known, it had little insight about the beginning of firearms, or how to cure disease.

Four Types:

Gestalt Examples: Leaves are like a tree, and so are you. The world may be yellow or blue. Everything is a beach, everything is a forest.

Opposition Examples: The strange one is different. All things separate for a time. Things come from the antipodes.

Quantity Examples: When one has happened, so has the other. The rule of the universal. Like to like. Things are often the same when there's more than one of the same --> Obviousness.

Motion Examples: Who knows? It will come. Something will happen.

Kenning was largely replaced after the medieval period, because of its reputation for superstition.

Systems Theory

MAGICAL SYSTEMS

ALCHEMY

Alchemy:

[Stages of, with an eye to immortality]

These levels suppose mostly linear progression of a spiritual order. Progress is possible in advanced areas first, but implies giftedness in those later areas, or neglect of the earlier ones.

1. Immutable Iron

2. Watery Birth

3. Quick Wood

4. Pure Milk

5. Crude Stone

6. Reflective Silver

7. Cleaning with Dirt

8. Crystal Clarity

9. Dreaming in Gold

10. Lengua Franca

11. Vital Root

12. Silver Tongue

13. Disillusionment

14. Work

15. Peace

16. Principle

17. Promise

18. Love

19. Happiness

20. Invulnerability

21. Prudence

22. Worldliness

23. Money

24. Feeling of mastery

25. Initiation

26. Occurrence

27. Mindfulness

28. Subtlety

29. Vitality

30. Characteristics

31. Minor Fame

32. Fitness

33. Occasional fortuity

34. Sometimes giftedness

35. Fertility

36. Minor Medicine

37. Crafting

38. Wit

39. Nobility

40. Familiarity

41. Rostrum: occult writings

42. Dictum: powerful language

43. Plebum: followers

44. Opii: miracles

45. Opii Mundi: vestiges

46. Essence (Virtue)

47. Corpus Regum (Secrets)

48. Aqua Vitae (Health)

49. Lapis (Astral Travel)

50. Subtil Effort (Magical Initiation)

51. Naming

52. Minor sooth-saying

53. Practicing Minor Arts

54. Control of Mana

55. Magical Lore

56. Magical Command

57. Magical Location

58. Select Minor Effects, such as:

    Magical Storage,

    Magical Manipulation, and

    Magical Strength,

59. Second Initiation: Occultation

60. Some Essential Effects:

    Friendship & Popularity,

    Increasing Confidence,

    Or, Sense of Mastery,

61. The Changeable World,

    Or, The Permanent World

62. Metaphysical validity

63. Test of Perfection

64. Engagement with Archetypes

65. Spiritual testing

Systems Theory

66. Trickery

   Or, Test of magical skill

67. Prolonged Mental Engagement

68. Immortal opportunity or folly

69. Treatment by a woman or man

70. Security

71. Hermeticism

72. Banishing demons

73. Innate Medical Knowledge

MAGICAL SYSTEMS

INCANTATIONS (OR MUTTERING)

This is a very traditional method of magic which goes back to at least the druidic period, or perhaps much earlier. It is related to a form of magic from Japan called 'Mudra' that has hand-signs some say could cause someone to change form into an animal, or do other kinds of magic. The traditional European form is basically directed magic, made possible by a silent incantation, such as silently muttered magic words. Sometimes this may be possible even without moving the mouth, making it a proper 'mind spell'. Here are some incantations for a variety of levels:

Level 1: 'Prufroc'

 Effect: Do something good

  for someone important.

Level 2: 'Myron Gyrin'

 Effect: Mindful choice amid chaos.

Level 3: 'A Moc d' Sade' and similar.

Effect: Control situations.

Level 4: 'Rumour patr siblair' and similar.

Effect: Gain the upper hand.

Level 5: 'Ex sensivus pax noisois'

Effect: Silence.

Level 6: 'Duribilis acumenicus troublanis mendicatus'

Effect: Clear worries / stupefy.

'Prodoxis Prodoxis' undoes this spell,

And is rumored to give infinite

knowledge.

Usually it just improves mindfulness.

(It is a spoken or silent spell, dissimilar

from muttered incantations).

MAGICAL SYSTEMS

CHI POWER

Eastern Magic:

Chi: Energy develops into Ki: Fire.

The following levels work if one has a powerful spiritual master such as Dynamo Jack (there is a video of him making a paper flame with his hands!).

Level 1: Practice these words:

"Everyone has chi"

"I give my body to chi"

Level 2: Have the grace of God. Do not be clumsy with your hands.

Be touched by the power of the master.

Level 3: Expand the field of energy. When in doubt, keep your hands low. Direct subtle energy long distances.

Level 4: Notice the invisible world. Grow in-tune with nature. Feel the electricity in your hands.

Systems Theory

General Background of Chinese Magic:

Elements: Gen (Magic), Wei (Energy), Wu (Space), Ki (Fire), and Doh (Art).

Gen is also translated as water.

Wei also means subtlety.

Wu (cloud) relates to Jiang (heaven): powers point towards heaven.

Ki is different from Wei in that one (Wei) is subtle, and the other Ki) is manifest. One only has as much ki as one can manifest.

Whereas, Wei is everywhere, unless the land is cursed.

Doh may also mean Tao or -Do, meaning training or immortal

way.

Thus, immortality and manifestation are on the outside. The body is subtle, and magic leads to heaven. The secret is in the clouds. The art is in the form. Fire consists of energy.

To get two, for example, to get the art of fire, you must get the other three: the art of fire comes from magical energy space. The art of energy comes from the magical space of fire. The art of magic comes from the energy space of fire. The greatest subtlety comes from the art of space, which is really the magical energy of fire. Do not believe that it is one thing or another: there is no difference between empty space and a folded flame! One can gain by another!

MAGICAL SYSTEMS

ENCHANTMENT

Sometimes called 'deep magic', enchantment comes in several traditions: [1] The tradition of magical incantation in which a particularly powerful object or person undergoes a significant change over the course of days, hours, or minutes. The same effect can be had by a god with greater agility. [2] The tradition of 'empty blessing' in which, for reasons that are magically concerned, a particular location experiences desirable weather for a time. This is close to priestly magic, and may be associated with a feeling of gladness. [3] The tradition of archaic or archana magic often written on papers or rocks. One example is the blessing to restore nets mentioned later. These spells may be larger explanations for reality than the reality which still exists, hence their power. [4] The tradition of living magic. Sometimes this is extended to include moving rocks, in addition to creating masses of stones or plants. [5] Bardic psychological magic may be tied to one of the other examples, or exist for its own effects. This may be rooted in Pan's rituals, the tradition of the Muses, or ancient queens and priestesses. [6] The magic of life and death, such as Brahma and the Egyptian Pharaohs, although rare, does sometimes exist. It may be called essentialist magic, and frequently has effects that are immediately visible with no source other than the power. These include powers to raise the dead---humans, animals, and plants---panacea, some variants of the elixir of life, and the ability to animate golems. Any effect which might depend on subtle ripples of space.

An enchantment used in mending nets:

"Socrates was formed of us,

And formed of us alacrity"

Systems Theory

The spell can be targeted using Eissel Tannon.

An enchantment for creating light:

'Pilfere Residuelis' (May require showing a narrow hole with the fingers to direct the light).

A spell for improving eyes and improving light in the room:

'Butter Charm… Butter CHARM'

Followed by: 'Mend Spice' which helps one to grasp hold of the shafts of light that are already in the room. This works with artificial light.

Enchanting Objects -]…Great advantages and great failures can be born from enchanting of objects. Most effects pass away almost immediately, but you may find that if an effect endures, it is like a family member. It is the thoughts like objectifying family members and not agreeing too much which seem frightening. But more often than not the wizard or witch lives alone, and could use some interesting company. The wizard or witch is of course something of a master or a fool with their possessions. Each of these characteristics should be used to the best effect.

MAGICAL SYSTEMS

WORMHOLES

The Wormhole of Medicine (L-Frames)

This is the type that might be observed during therapy. Why don't other people in the world look or act like me? Maybe it's because of one of these! For example,

"Guess what? They do special things for ADD";

Unfortunately for you, typically you can't remember that someone ever said this. After all the disease you ended up having wasn't ADD. Maybe you fell through the wormhole of medicine.

Time-Travel Wormholes

This method uses a rule of similarity between the points of travel to create a 'synergasm' or invisible wormhole between the two involved worlds... There may be no major similarity between the two corresponding worlds other than a temporary temporal similarity. To travel to the past you may need a horcrux. To travel to the future you need to be psychic.

Systems Theory

MAGICAL SYSTEMS

AURA READING

Spritely, arrogant: Red

Dark, cold, intellectual: Blue

Seems pink or red at first: Yellow

Seems to stare at you, fashionable: Black

Hard to read, good impression: White or Grey

Impressive and sloppy or draws your attention in: Purple

MAGICAL SYSTEMS

PSYCHIC PREDICTION

FORMS OF PSYCHIC PREDICTION

Psychic prediction may take several basic forms.

First I will describe the most basic types of prediction.

First of all, the most basic type is 0-dimensional prediction. This consists of predicting what has already occurred, that is, predicting the types of things that have already happened. A second degree of this is had by predicting things that are similar to those things that have happened. For our purposes, this can be called simple generalization. If Henrick usually wants to play games, perhaps he wants to play games now. This is the first dimension of prediction, and it is the type that gains most easily by probabilistic inductions. This method is also called specialized prediction when it is applied to specialized modes of behavior. For example, we can predict that a Matisse will sell high compared to an unknown artist. We know that popular items in an auction sell high, whereas unpopular items might not sell at all. Therefore, there is an exponential relationship for example, between selling a Matisse, and selling a Matisse at an auction. These kinds of things can be predicted by studying the specific character of the modalities and events involved in a given situation. However, if an event is instead informal or contrived, this lends an aspect of unpredictability. The predictions only work when all of the prior conditions are met, and become less predictable with every difference from the previous cases. Therefore, differences can be used to predict differences, as another type of specialized prediction. It may help to predict trickery or confusion ('likely outcomes'), rather than predicting a specific event. It should be accepted that some conditions and choices are arbitrary. Because we do not know if conditions will be met to satisfaction, we know that some events are arbitrary. If the conditions are one half different, then prediction requires a strong degree of formalism, however that is calculated. It involves, in effect, exceeding expectations, or coming across an event that happened just in the same way, but as if by chance. This is one reason that scientists have been known to require the reproduction of laboratory conditions, even with highly predictable phenomena. Thus, specialized predictions have some limitations.

The next type is delineative or elaborative prediction. What it consists of is a generalization modified by additional imagination about the significance of the factors involved. This type of prediction can be called variablistic, because it often functions by applying a generalization to a deduction about a variable. If elephants are painted red, perhaps it is a sight for sore eyes, etc. One form of this is prediction through emergence. This is not necessarily a linear prediction because it essentially doesn't predict based on existing data. Nor does it predict based on known exterior data. Instead, it involves a conclusion that something is missing from the data. Logical conclusions are drawn so that we can make major systemic conclusions about what the data means. The new theory appears as if from thin air. This is similar to the emergence of Darwinism, or the genetic explanation of reproduction. What determines the success of these theories is their relative importance, not necessarily the lack of any alternative. It is the importance of the theory----its

emergence----which drives the prediction. (Many theories from

social science involve emergent theories, such as socialism and

capitalism. Instead of acting as a formal constraint, they often

expand the way that the conditions function. In this case, the

explanation is not erroneous, but instead, serves as a new

rational mode of explanation).

A third type is contingent or categorical prediction. If something

is the case, then we can predict that the things that rely upon this

first condition are modified when that category is modified. This

form of prediction works better for predicting quality differences

than actually-different conditions. However, if multiple qualities

are absent, predictions can be made about the alternatives. If

there is no snow, it can be predicted that it is not cold, or there is

a shortage of water, for instance. If it is not cold, one can predict

that it is arid or moist. If there is a shortage of water, one can

predict that it is dry, or there is a high tolerance for water. This

can also take the form of complex categorization. Attaching

variables to a given object means that predicting the outcome for

the main object affects the outcome of some, if not all, of the variables. For example, 'if we do something extreme, the change might be observable. Otherwise, it is an abstract or un-measurable form of extremity. We must have some means of observation, or we can usually conclude that the effects are not extreme. Or we can adopt an irrational view'.

A fourth type of prediction is coherent prediction. This is also called synergism or epiphany. The simplest form of coherent prediction occurs by the exclusion of all but one unlikely option. Hella spent a hot day in the desert, and she was outdoors, and walked several miles, time passed and she didn't expire: she must have brought something to drink with her. A more complex form occurs by qualifying what it means to make a given combination. People who have complicit sex are always lovers. Therefore, if two people have sex, it might be complicit, and they might be lovers. Or, something is complicit between two people. If it is sex, they are lovers. This can even involve highly complex phenomena. For example: Joe defines himself as an editor, but he works as an economist. In some way he is doing economic editing. This is the beginning of a genuinely psychic method. Attaching judgments of fully embraced variables can be a meaningful way of reaching for epiphanies. For example, what 'definitely IS something' about a given thing? Then apply that condition to factors like responsibility, organization, and predictability. An exception to this is so-called 'black swans'. In that case, one must predict the rationale which makes something a black swan. The rule in that case is that things are either unreasonable, reasonable, without purpose, or serving a prescribed function. A method for solving black swans involves corroboration or defaulting. This occurs when there is no better explanation remaining for a given thing. Well, we know that such-and-such a creature has eyes based on the related species, but nothing about the creature looks exactly like eyes. The eyes must be these spots on its back. Otherwise its blind. Or, black swans could exist, as long as we know that color serves no inherent function.

Now for more genuine psychic predictions:

A second genuine form of psychic prediction involves using a posteriori reasoning on a 0-dimensional prediction. For example, if we know that some events are arbitrary, then we can derive that we don't know if some conditions will be met to satisfaction.

If we know Henrick wants to play games now, we can predict that he usually wants to play games. This form of prediction often involves deducing the types of statements that lead to a particular line of reasoning: that is, predicting a rationale. Many psychics are familiar with this way of phrasing deductions.

A third form of genuine psychic prediction involves determination based on unstated facts. Since everyone thinks about the opposite of what they say, at least unconsciously, combining multiple opposite terms for terms that have been stated as someone's opinion, or as the definition of a motive or interest for the person or organization, will give information about the genuine motivations, or else the looming unknowns in the life of the person or organization. For example, if someone states that the first thing on their mind is their motorcycle, and the second thing on their mind is their manhood, then you can predict that they're concerned about meeting someone else on a motorcycle.

A fourth form of genuine psychic prediction involves categorical relationships. One can ask or predict 'what is someone's usual mode of relation with the world?' Then one can predict that they use that mode of relation with their perceived opposites. For example, an artist who expresses that the thing on his mind is cars can be predicted 'not to buy a painting of a car, instead you'll make it yourself' (the concealed opposition is between the artist who makes art, and his opposite, the buyer of the art. The opposite of making a painting of a car is buying a painting of a car). Similarly, if a business expresses itself as aggressive and competitive, but you think they're liars, you can predict they'll have contradictory marketing ('competing truths', since their mode of relation is competition, and their opposite is the truth).

A fifth form of genuine psychic prediction: take any number of factors describing a current event or situation you're in, and reverse the factors that are different from the subject. This can be used to predict how someone is feeling, or what their core motivation are. For example, an artist is at a business convention. So they're feeling unconventional, and they feel like making art, since that is not a different motive from business. Or, a philosophy society is at an art gallery. So, it thinks its popular art ('society' does not conflict with 'gallery'), and it thinks its un-philosophical art, or tries to make connections between art and

363

philosophy ('philosophy' is different from 'art' or it can be

debated). Other conclusions might be that they think art is trying

to commercialize philosophy, that philosophy ought to involve

graphics, or to view art or philosophy as a socialist movement.

Those are the eight categories of prediction that I have

determined. I hope this writing may be considered useful to my

readers on this most often unrealized subject.

Works Cited

Coppedge, Nathan. The Dimensional Psychologist's Toolkit.
CSIP, 2014

Systems Theory

MAGICAL SYSTEMS

"OBJECTS OF INFLUENCE"

Symbolic objects such as cards, talismans, paintings, engraved furniture etc. is either real or false, and should be considered for Its perfection, and be devoid of negativity. Unstable objects like rickety shelves and balances can be used to test the power of a symbolic object in question, such as a medical textbook.

Symbols of power mean something against everyone who does

not possess such symbols.

Many objects such as comforts and luxuries add to the power of

symbols, by reinforcing their legitimacy (providing a context for

appreciating them, and therefore, taking them seriously).

The strongest political domains thus have comforts, put negative

symbols into question, possess symbols of power, and make

positive use of symbols.

MAGICAL SYSTEMS

MAGICAL RUMINATION

Sometimes known as Love or Christianity.

Is essentially the collection of past and present objects and persons and worlds and spells and their correlations.

Further concepts:

*Origination: a world may begin with a spell, or a person with an

object, or a spell with a person, etc.

*The Sacred Heart: people become like God when they do not

taint themselves with false promises.

*The Humble Soul: the soul can think, and in this process,

creates divine correlations.

*Rumination: is the ability to feel and live within the realm of souls, hearts, and origins. Rumination takes place as a way of sensing higher dimensions of existence, and also of communing through the process of love, such as sensing the auras of nearby persons or objects.

Systems Theory

MAGICAL SYSTEMS

APOCRYPHAL PROPHECY

The first aspect is to nail the concept of how to express passages of time.

For example, by saying "In the First Age...".

Or, "After an uncertain number of years..."

These initial decisions provide structure for the system of prophecy.

For example, if X happens in the First Age, one can apply a theory such as evolution, transcendentalism, cultural degeneration, etc. to reach Y in the Second Age. If one can predict the same pattern, then one can predict Z in the Third Age, or U in the Fourth Age, etc.

However, if the theory of prophecy is wrong, the prediction will also be wrong.

Therefore, it is important for the theory of prophecy to fit one of the following criteria:

1. The results follow logically.

2. The theory is sufficiently vague that it remains probable. This can be helped by working with existing information.

3. The prediction is psychic. See Psychic Prediction.

4. The prediction works with classical knowledge of history, psychology, theology, or politics such as knowledge of the gods or

bodies of immortal literature.

Systems Theory

MAGICAL SYSTEMS

PREMONITION / ADMONISHMENT

The wise grow weary of the world,

Unless they are held enchanted.

Innocence is soon lost.

Witnessing destruction has a cost.

Gaining and losing is a loss, particularly when the souls die.

Experience and wisdom come at great expense.

The ways of the world pass away.

When one grows old one may have few friends.

Time immemorial tells many tales,

But they are bound up in one story.

Avail yourselves of the good power,

And do not let your body pass into debilitation.

MAGICAL SYSTEMS

MYSTERIES

Perfection rises above the mein.

Silence is full of meaning.

The body (hands, arms) are a figure of design.

The mind is an amalgamation of facts of great value.

The psychik gives instructions on reality.

The metaphysician is the master-doctor, available to all.

God is a power that emerges naturally.

Wishes are sacred thinking.

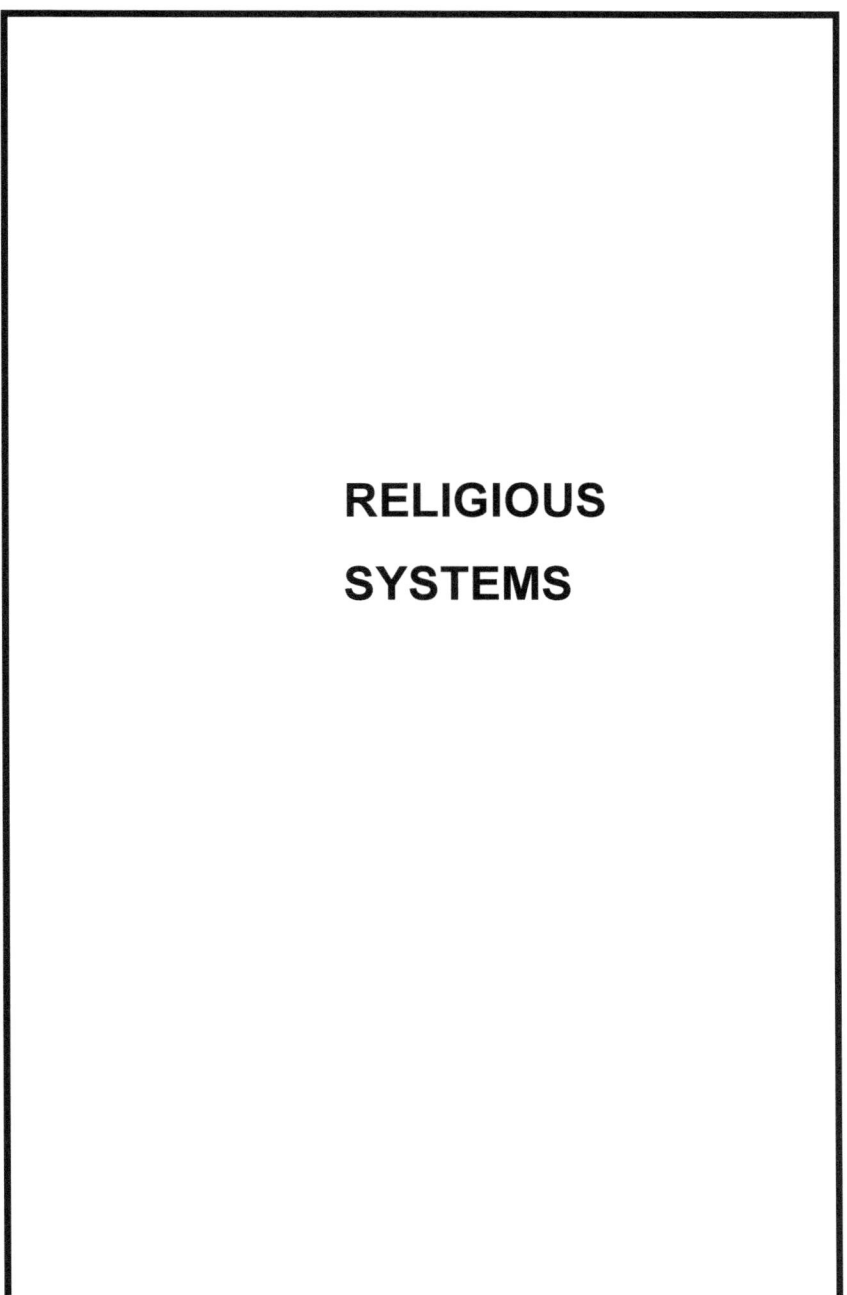

RELIGIOUS

SYSTEMS

Systems Theory

RELIGIOUS SYSTEMS

ASCETICISM

Perhaps the first esotericism, asceticism sprung from the practice of bodily health coming from the instinct for self-preservation, as well as the practice of extreme temperance resulting from the cautionary relinquishing of worldly experiences.

An ascetic (the practitioner of asceticism) is often a hermit, yogi, shaman, or monk who adopts a harsh or abstemious lifestyle as part of a principled set of beliefs of personal or worldly denial.

Sometimes asceticism springs from real or exaggerated regret about worldly experiences, as in the case of Siddhartha Gautama ("The Buddha"), or modern Buddhists.

Modern life has provided fewer and fewer opportunities for real asceticism, at least in the sense of a hermit in the mountains. Life is more technologically inter-connected than ever before, and this reduces the status of the ascetic lifestyle.

Some now feel the same profundity about a fruit smoothie as they once did about an ascetic lifestyle. In the midst of warfare enforced by governments, it begins to seem arbitrary whether pleasure is wrong, or just sometimes impractical. However, the ascetic lifestyle remains a strong representation of what it means to have moderation and strong principles.

Not only have artificial images of master teachers become common, but asceticism now involves navigating through many false representations of the meaning of renunciation.

For most spiritual practitioners, this has meant a movement towards moderation.

Systems Theory

RELIGIOUS SYSTEMS

EPICUREANISM AND HEDONISM

An early example of alternatives to the strict ascetic lifestyle is

represented by Epicurus (341 - 270 BC).

Epicurus advised a lifestyle of moderate pleasures in which pain,

importantly, was to be avoided.

Some consider his viewpoint to be contradictory, since indul-gence

without another principle of virtue might lead to suffering.

In more recent history, the availability of sugar, caffeine, and

other drugs, as well as increase in the availability of luxuries has

made abstention from pleasure seem more and more pointless,

and this has led to a rise in the popularity of Hedonistic beliefs.

Although Epicurus was closer to the moderate beliefs of Aris-totle, hedonists such as Bentham argued that pleasure was the means

to oppose pain, and thus, it was pointless to avoid extreme

indulgences.

In my own theories I argue that pleasure is simply different from

pain: pleasure is karma from good information, and pain is simply

a symptom of total dysfunctionality. In this way, the relation is

indirect enough not to justify a move away from moderate

beliefs.

RELIGIOUS SYSTEMS

ASCETICUREANISM

"The realization of a perception is like a pile of stones." ---

Asceticurus

"Each person is god of themselves"

---Asceticurus

"True religion is for the gods. The religion of mortals is called

spirituality."

---Asceticurus

"Matter is meaning in whatever form it takes"

---Asceticurus

FOUNDING TEXTS OF ASCETICUREANISM

INCLUDE THE METAPHYSICAL ART

WHICH CAN BE FOUND UNDER AESTHETICS

See also The Spiritual Writings by Nathan Coppedge / Asceticurus.

EXTRA-
PROGRAMM-
ABLE
SYSTEMS

PROGRAMMABLE SYSTEMS

OBJECT-ORIENTED PROGRAMMING

The scenario defines the actors, but the scenario is just a string of rooms presented as dialogue. "W"—> "enter room 1" etc.

Entified actors are actors that do actions. Actions are responses to user-input. Every actor and object is a compound of all the categories that overlap with it, a process called inheritance.

Sometimes inheritance may change, creating exchanges. Therein lies the complexity. Dialogues permit changes in the variables which define the relations of objects and actors. Dialogues are mediated by 'daemons', which are programs delegated to perform a specific task.

The earlier types often relate with Actors, Daemons, and Variable-Dialogue (the properties and verbs of actors). Depending on how objects are interpreted, object-oriented programming may have different philosophies, for example, the value of actors-as-objects (alien phenomenology), on 'scenes' which are compounds of daemons (object-oriented religion), or on dialogues and variables (Neo-Classical objectivity), and so on. The fourth tends to be something high-minded like aesthetic or coherent approaches..

PROGRAMMABLE SYSTEMS

COHERENT LOGIC PROGRAM

Extending a theory of proof vs. unfounded, quality vs. property, opp / opp, and system / n-operator, valid vs. incompetent logics.

The following is designed for a simple computer program. The most complex aspect is if you want to make the process flow better, by cataloguing all the opposites in the English language with opposite matching, so that the matching is done automatically.

1A. Is what you are considering a paradox?

{1 term: Not a paradox!

2 terms: If opposite terms: you've come to the end of knowledge!

3 terms: Exceptional paradox!

4 terms: If your terms are terms are all opposites, the answer can

be absolute! If your opposite terms are in opposite positions, your

Systems Theory

problem can be stated as absolute knowledge.}

General method of Paroxysm

What is a term necessary for the problem?

Do you want to add / delete any terms?

Then the solution to paradox with terms (x, y, z ....) is the paroxysm with terms (opp x, opp y, opp z...)

Does this answer the problem?

If Y, then:

Do you want to save the solution?

1B. Is what you are considering a problem?

Do you want a general solution?

--> What is the problem?

[One word answer --> Can you be more specific (restate if necessary?)]

-->The ultimate solution to 'X Problem' is 'Opp X solution' which is short for 'a solution to Opp X'.

Was that helpful?

If no, how about a solution to Opp X? [Skip to frequent answers].

2A. Do you want help with an existing solution?

What are the two best terms of the solution? (x, y)

Is it X? No, then Y.

Is it Y? No, then X.

Systems Theory

If it is neither, then you have a paradox [Go to Paradoxes].

If it is X and Y:

"Then you may have a problem".

Do any of the terms serve as solutions?

Yes? Then apply them!

No? Then, do you want a general solution? (above).

3A. Do you have a philosophical problem?

-->Then pick two pairs of opposites that refer to your problem.

-->Which word of the four is most important? (-->A)

-->Then quality A (B) as related to quality C (D) AND / OR

quality A (D) as related to quality C (B) will constitute knowledge on the subject.

4A. Do you have a systems question?

Neutral, balanced, infinite --> Coherent.

Neutral, balanced, finite --> Modular.

Neutral, imbalanced, infinite --> Essence, History.

Neutral, imbalanced, finite --> Insight.

Asymmetric, balanced, infinite --> Degeneration.

Asymmetric, balanced, finite --> Functions.

Asymmetric, imbalanced, infinite --> Form.

Asymmetric, imbalanced, finite --> Observations.

The above is also available as an academic article at: https://www.academia.edu/15428200/Logics Seeking comments and implementation for Javascript.

Further information on coherency theory may be found at: The Logic of Coherence. And elsewhere on the Main Systems Theory Page.

Systems Theory

ADDITIONAL NOTES ON COHEENT LOGIC PROGRAM:

CATEGORICAL DEDUCTION-RELATED WRITINGS

Arbitrary / Paroxysmal Deduction ('Just' Deduction):

1-d:

A then D

D then A

(A and D are opposites)

2-d:

'AB' is 'CD'

'BC' is 'DA'

'CD' is 'AB'

'DA' is 'BC'

Basically two deductions.

A and C are opposite, B and D are opposite.

similar to categorical deduction or

two-part paroxysm.

3-d:

'ABC' is 'DEF'

'BCD' is 'EFA'

'CDE' is 'FAB'

'DEF' is 'ABC'

'EFA' is 'BCD'

'FAB' is 'CDE'

Basically three deductions.

A and D are opposite.

B and E are opposite.

C and F are opposite.

4-d:

'A conj B boolean* C conj D' OR

'A conj D boolean* C conj B'

the statement is justice of / just as:

'opp A conj opp B Opp boolean** opp C conj opp D' OR

'opp A conj opp D Opp boolean** opp C conj opp B'

Basically four deductions.

(The opposites can be nouns or adjective forms.

C must be the opposite of A,

and D must be the opposite of B).

*(for example, 'and' / 'or' / 'always' / 'never'

'rarely' / 'usually')

*(for example, 'or' / 'and' / 'never' / 'always' /

'usually' / 'rarely')

Opp Boolean must be opposite of Boolean in this case,

so the Boolean operators cannot be neutral.

Standard Categorical Deduction:

'A conj B Neutral Boolean* C conj D'

'A conj D Neutral Boolean* C conj B'

Two deductions strictly in terms of A.

Preference is given to the first and second terms.

Otherwise determined.

The second terms retain the same logic regardless of preference.

A and C are opposite.

B and D are opposite.

Conjunction of terms is primary.

*(for example 'is' , 'as is' , 'just as' , 'when' , 'so', 'and as such')

Paroxysm:

problem 'ABC...' --> solution 'oppA oppB oppC...'

similar to 3-part deduction, except quantity of terms is explicitly

flexible.

again, accepts noun or adjective terms.

in this case, conjunction of terms is secondary.

Deduction Using Unconventional Opposites

complexity/perfection/arbitration/ambiguity A --->

perfection/complexity/ambiguity/arbitration opposite A

This is a hand-holding version of categorical deduction

in which specific less common comparisons are preferred

for half of the deduction.

E.g. A is equivalent here to B in standard deductions.

Opposite A is equivalent to D in standard deductions.

A selection is made between A and C, so B and D need

not be selected again.

Systems Theory

PROGRAMMABLE SYSTEMS

BRANDING PROGRAM

What is the primary keyword?

Is it 'Genius', 'Functionality', 'Pleasure', or 'Dangerous'?

If none of these words fit, just pick one of them and it will work as a brand.

If you want the brand to be more specific, then use the following rules:

Regardless of the keyword chosen,

    A. Set 1: Generic form.

        1. Apply a related proper name that has not been branded.

            A. Optional: If there is little to no competition

            choose amongst this set of words:

                [New, Quality, Evolution, or number of units]

        2. Modify the name so that it is unique.

        3. Add additional unique property words.

For example, Coppedge Car = Cooper Mini.

B. Set 2: Technical variations

1. In the case of highly technical products, what does the keyword signify. Pick anything that fits, such as a recent discovery, or unique design. These can be other keywords specific to thepro-duct, or simply creative words that capture something about the design. For example, 'Ninja Broom' or 'Elementary Discovery'.

2. If there is no unique qualifier, pick a tradi-tional related category of genius, and add a prefix, such as Hyper-, Uber-, Meta-, Ultra- etc. If the name is a new brand, stop here. For example, 'Hyper-Cubism'.

3. If the name is not yet a brand, add a word describing the thing's function. For example, Uber-Ultra Soap, or Hyper-Categorical Frame-works.

Some brand names arrived at by a similar method include:

Cooper Mini, Eb Lens, Hyper-Cubism, Paroxysm, Bobbi's Market, Alchemy Club, Categorical Deduc-tion, quasi-feminist sculpture by a man, Evolution Tattoos, and Keys on Kites Tattoos.

Systems Theory

PROGRAMMABLE SYSTEMS

ANCIENT BOOK DESIGN PROGRAM

SECRET BOOKS FORMULA

Soul of the book =

   If you [X] qualifier [subject of x and qualifier] [opp X clarified]

Optionally, you can add a moral:

 It is [Substantiality of X] to [verb / adj. of opp qualifier].

Title of book =

Usually: [quality of X] [opp of qualifier found in soul]

For quick use: [opp of qual. found in soul] [quality of X]

The easiest way to use the formula is to generate original souls

and then find the corresponding titles by finding the most

essential, knowledgeable quality of X and then finding the

opposite of the qualifier introduced in the soul of the book.

Together with the soul the title provides a basic index of the value

of any text, and permits exponentially efficient reading.

For example,

Soul = 'If you die early enough you live'.

Optional 1= 'Death is the aging process'.

Title of book = 'Bad Archaic'

Bad [= qual. of die] Archaic [=opp of early]

Another example chosen more arbitrarily,

Soul = 'If you live surely truth may die'

Optional 1= 'The life is uncertain'.

Title of book = 'Optimal Uncertainty'

Optimal [=qual. of live] Uncertainty [= opp of surely]

For additional examples of souls of literature,

See: nathancoppedge.com/alexandria.html

PROGRAMMABLE SYSTEMS

SCRIPTED FUNCTIONS

There is a different approach to functions depending on the modus operandi. For example, if functions are 'poisoned' then one wants to use the fewest possible functions to achieve some effect. If the effect is unlikely, one may have to minimize cost, or minimize effect.

On the other hand, if the functions are exponential, then there might be no risk, or it might be advantageous to have expert advice on combining functions.

If the function must be related to an existing system or function, then it is important to 'tailor' the function to fit the existing modality.

If the function must be utilitarian, then the focus should be on maximizing the good effects of the function, and streamlining implementation, with an eye towards the advantage of repeated iterations of improvements.

Generally, the advantage is always expressed in terms of functions of whatever type.

contact [at] nathancoppedge.com for any systems
suggestions

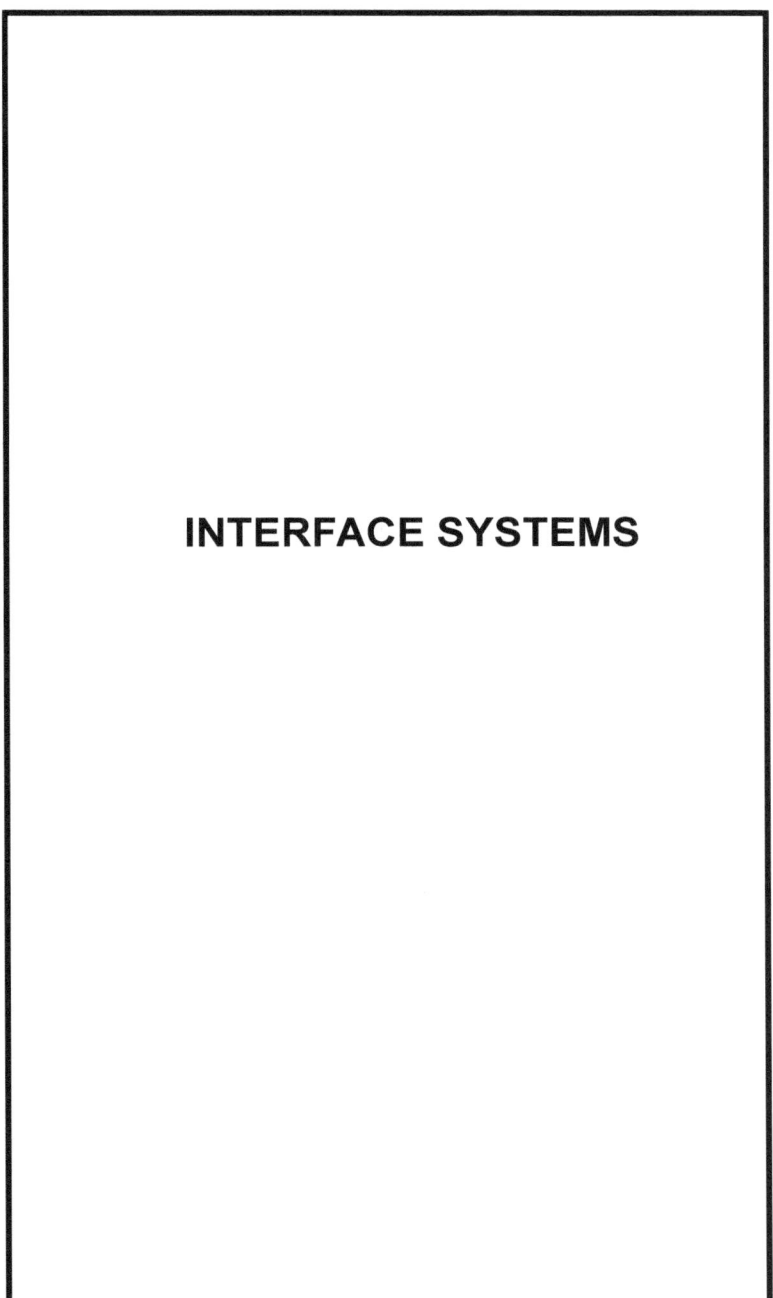

INTERFACE SYSTEMS

Systems Theory

INTERFACE SYSTEMS

OPEN-AND-CLOSED LOGICS

An open-and-shut system essentially works to reinforce a pre-existing function or provide secondary rhetorical support for a system. It works within the assumptions already present in the system, and returns the same argument or standards already existing within the system.In its archetypal form it may follow 2 - 4 steps, which adopt the following rules:

If it follows 4 steps, the logic supports the entirety of a system whose function is generally taken-for-granted. For example, it may provide additional explanations of something previously unexplained, typically through cycles such as cycles of nature. Thus, the first of three types of open-and-shut systems is a circular process that serves an explanatory function.

If it follows 3 steps it is often not natural, but metaphysical. One extreme case is considered, with its natural extension, but another opposite extreme case is introduced leading back to the original argument. This may be seen as a dialectical argument often with the effect of supporting the least contested system.

If it follows 2 steps it is often not natural or metaphysical, but transcendental. The first of the two steps involves special insight into the subject, while the second step involves its natural conclusion, often some form of godhood or epiphany. Like the immediately-previously mentioned type, it may serve as a more efficient shortcut to longer-step methods.The insight of the method is that typologically 1-category sets and 5-category sets would be considered identical, which is the notional premise.Open-and-shut arguments divide reality into: (1) knowledge, (2) arguments, and (3) intelligence. And they output just these things.

Nathan Coppedge

INTERFACE SYSTEMS

EXPANSION MODELS

This is a one-two methodology.

Expensive systems begins with far-ranging logic, such as the remains of a universe, or sparse information. The data is expensive because it is gathered from the furthest reaches, the furthest sources. The best data / physics etc. is found within it, and is used as a beginning-point for new formalism.

Expansive systems begin with a condensed state such as that found at the beginning of a creative project, and implement repetitions or variations of the best data / physics as found in the expensive model. The data is expansive because it works with a small but highly qualified initial model to create a larger project.

Collectively, what is provided is a universal model of expansion.

INTERFACE SYSTEMS

WATERING-HOLE STRATEGIES

If a precondition is 'poisoned' with some specific property of advantageousness, then it can be seen that the strategy, if there is a strategy, that evolves from that application, expresses itself in terms of the initial conditions of the 'watering-hole', and all the real-life conditions that expand from that initial 'seeding'.

So, in the second place, the limit is the presence of any type of anti-poison or incapacitation of the application, and the utility of the application is its adoption by other, perhaps wildly different watering-hole equivalencies. Some of these secondary elements may follow a pattern similar to the original, and either communicate or fail to communicate the 'poison'. The poison then dissipates, or becomes incorporated in the structure of the 'wells'.

However, what happens when the source of the 'poison' was very distant, and aimed to gain advantages by the poison? What is its strategy to recover the poison in an altered form?

One strategy might be to motivate the first 'well' to evolve in some way, and then find a comfortable position amongst the resulting much larger evolutions. This seemingly would require already being evolved. Another strategy would be to create a hard-to-understand 'poison' and adapt gradually to the resulting drama and education.

In general, the strategy would be to anticipate the effect of the 'poison' and find assurance that the effect was advantageous.

Nathan Coppedge

APPENDIX

Nathan Coppedge

APPENDIX 1

Basic Structure

1. Information

2. Aphorisms

3. Objective Knowledge

4. Solution to Paradoxes

5. Formula for Souls

Nathan Coppedge

END OF MAIN TEXT

RECOMMENDED READING BY NATHAN COPPEDGE

The Golden Notebook
*The Dimensional Book of
    Quotations*
*Properties, Systems, Paths,
    and Levels*
Psychological Knowledge
*Psychic Prediction
    Techniques*
The Book of Ideas
Coherent Systems Theory

SERIES

*The Dimensional Encyclope-
dia*
*The Perpetual Motion Genius'
Guides*
Asceticurean Writings

Systems Theory

BIO

Nathan Coppedge, (b. 1982) is a philosopher, artist, inventor, and poet in some capacity. He is a famous quotable on Poemhunter and a member of the International Honor Society for Philosophy. He has been quoted on Book Forum and in the Hartford Courant. He is an abstract modern artist and runs a website on systems theory and perpetual motion machines. He is responsible for the development of the methods of non-causal inference, paroxysm, and a method for auto-generating the souls of literature. He has also played a role in suggesting corporate brand names to companies such as Eb Lens, Cooper Mini, and Alchemy Club.

www.ingramcontent.com/pod-product-compliance
Lightning Source LLC
Chambersburg PA
CBHW071326280526
45787CB00001B/8